A Life Spiritually Guided by Faith, Daisies, and Sky-Blue Pink

A Personal Journey through Childhood, Love, and Loss

KL Nelson

ISBN 979-8-88540-220-0 (paperback)
ISBN 979-8-88540-265-1 (hardcover)
ISBN 979-8-88540-221-7 (digital)

Christian Faith Publishing
832 Park Avenue
Meadville, PA 16335
www.christianfaithpublishing.com

Printed in the United States of America

To my sons,

I pray you will learn to let faith be your guide in life. I hope you will find your perfect love, and I wish for you strength through the Lord. You will always be the greatest treasures in my life, and I will forever be with you among the daisies and the skies of blue and pink.

Acknowledgments

If there were ever a truth in this world that meant more to me, it is the truth of God and His presence in my life, all of my life. I am blessed to have had parents who chose to put in the effort to send me to a Christian school that taught me the values I hold so dear to my heart today and allowed me to find God and carry Him with me throughout my life.

To my parents, thank you for looking beyond yourselves, seeing what was best for me, and giving me a treasure in my life that can never be measured in words.

For most everyone, there is a person who came into your life or was a part of your life growing up who meant everything to you and instilled a great piece of who you are into your being; for me, there were two, my grandmother and my great-grandmother. These two women gave to me unconditional love and affection, but they also guided me and taught me to value myself, carry myself with dignity and grace, have respect for myself, and hold strong to my faith in God.

My grandmothers showed me that if I looked within myself and allowed my heart and mind to be freely open, I could see, hear, and feel the path ahead of me through God and the Holy Spirit surrounding me.

To my grandmothers, I cherish you more than you could ever know, and I look forward to the moment we reunite and embrace the forever after together. Thank you for your wisdom and grace.

I will forever be thankful for my sweet husband, the amazing man he was, and the joy he brought to my life, not just through him but through our incredible four boys that together we cherish and adore. My children have been my rock since my husband's passing and continue to be my strength. My husband always believed I was stronger than I knew myself to be, and he always pushed me to aim higher for myself in my career and my belief in me. He was a strong man, a loving man, and I will always love him.

To my husband, thank you for believing in me and giving me strength and courage when I felt self-doubt. Thank you for loving me. I cannot wait to share eternity with you.

To my children, I am immensely proud of the men you are today; and if you take anything with you throughout your life, let it be your faith in God and the open mind to let God lead you on your path. Thank you for picking me up when life seemed hopeless and always bringing joy to my life. I will forever be grateful for having been blessed with the gift of being your mother.

To my Lord and Savior, thank you for seeing in me what I could not see in myself and for leading me when I called upon you to take the wheel. My heart is full, knowing you are with me always.

Finally, to my friends and family who have been my cheerleaders and have inspired me to take my writing further, thank you for your encouragement, your love, and your faith in me. It truly means the world.

Chapter 1

It was a beautiful, warm, sunny day, walking steps behind my mother and her friend as we strolled through the strawberry field filling our baskets with fresh strawberries plucked from the vine. Not every strawberry picked made it into my basket; a few tempted me to eat them, and joyously I did.

It was on this day that I was first enlightened by a spirit from a past life. We had arrived back at the house of my mother's friend and had just finished a late lunch. I had stepped away from the table to play on my own when suddenly a female presence appeared that only I could see. She was an elderly woman, small and plump in stature. She wore a crimson scarf with dainty white eyelet flowers softly wrapped around her gentle face, which seemed to glow with a warm smile as she stood in front of me holding a small basket filled with bright beams of yellow flowers. I did not know why she was there, but just the same, I felt the desire to place a nearby scarf over my head and proceeded to hum to myself as I gingerly wobbled around the room, just as I believed she would have carried herself had she made the slightest sound or moved at all.

I must have been quite the spectacle because, at that moment, my mother asked, "Who are you supposed to be?"

Without any hesitation, as if I had known her all my life, I stated, "I am Peshka Gustaff!" I never understood why she appeared to me that day, but for whatever reason, I have never forgotten her face or her name, and it is a story my mother never stops telling.

I was always a quiet little girl who was content to play on my own. All of my stuffed animals were my friends and were forced to take part in my make-believe world. I found myself teaching them Bible verses and reading to them from the Bible and other books as I played teacher in a classroom of bears, puppy dogs, and rag dolls. There were also times when I would play at a friend's house, or they would play at mine.

On one such occasion, while visiting a friend, we decided to play "house" with our baby dolls. While I have no recollection as to why our imaginations led us in this direction, we pretended to be married to drunkard men; and when it came time for them to come home, we would take our babies into another room, not wanting to be around them while in that state of mind. While playing, the feelings I was pretending to have toward my pretend drunken husband suddenly felt all too real, and I immediately told my friend I did not want to play this way anymore. For me, what I was feeling was very discomforting and seemed eerily familiar. We never played that version of "house" again. This would be my first childhood premonition, an insight into feelings I would hold later on in my life.

I was not really sure why these off-kilter moments happened to me back then. Over time, I've learned that some of us are blessed through God's will and that spirits of lost souls reach out to those who are blessed in order to connect their souls to paradise, and for some, premonitions occur in order for them to do His work here on earth. As I got older, I slowly started to gain acceptance for the spiritual moments I was experiencing. It all started with my grandmothers.

Two of the most important figures in my life were my maternal great-grandmother and grandmother. They were both gentle, loving women of faith and full of wisdom, and I was blessed to have them share their wisdom with me.

My grandmothers always spoke of premonitions and spirits that came to them and how they believed it was for the Lord's purpose. It was through them and the lessons in private school that I found God and learned that He is always with me, and if I allow him to lead, I will find strength through Him, and he will provide me with the answers I continue to seek—He will never let me fall. My grandmothers always told me, "God will never give you anything you cannot handle."

My parents could never know the impact it made leaving me with my grandmothers for long evenings on their date nights. We shared club crackers, orange juice with a teaspoon of sugar—of course, to cut the acid—brown sugar fudge (my great-grandmother's personal recipe, the best in my opinion), and Whitman's chocolates. We always watched *The Glen Campbell Music Show*, and I would lay across their laps, loving every precious moment we had together—three of four generations sharing priceless time.

I have never seen two more beautiful women in my life. As a young girl, I was blessed to be laying across both of these graceful beauties, one stroking my hair and the other softly rubbing my back while they shared with me their thoughts on how a woman should carry herself, and the strength she holds by acting with dignity and grace.

My great-grandmother was the epitome of grace and beauty. She had the whitest hair, soft like cotton, and even in her nineties, she had the most beautiful figure almost like an angel. She was sweet but stern and held more love in her pinky finger than most could hold in a lifetime.

She was always teaching me to be a lady. One of the fondest memories I have of her shared wisdom was when she instructed me, "Young lady, have respect for yourself. Always remember to turn off the light before undressing. A man should never see you in your God-given form but should hold his love for you by the person you are within."

My husband and I would chuckle about this years later, but I always understood and respected her point.

One night when I was ten years old, sudden gentle pressure on the side of my bed awakened me as if someone had just sat beside me. As I turned over to see who was there, I was awestruck by the beauty before me. My great-grandmother was sitting at my bedside, her hand placed gently on my arm. Her face looked so young, and the hair draped across her shoulders was the brightest white with subtle hints of gold. She was gracefully wrapped in a long, flowing white gown, and there was a glow all around her. She just seemed to sit there, softly smiling at me, and then slowly leaned forward and kissed my cheek, and within an instant, she was gone.

The very next morning, my mother came to my room weeping and shared with me that my great-grandmother had passed away and had taken her place in heaven. It was at that very moment that I realized this was why she had come to me—she was saying goodbye.

Seeing my great-grandmother in such a state of beauty when she appeared beside me left me feeling comforted with her death, and I knew she would always be with me.

It would not come with such grace and comfort when my grandmother passed away ten years later. It was one of the worst moments in my life.

As a young girl, my mother was in and out of the hospital quite often and at one point almost died from a misguided surgery. Because of this, my grandmother spent a lot of time taking care of me and being the mother figure in my life, and she always called me her angel. If you ask me, my grandmother was the sweetest, most-endearing woman you could ever know, and nobody could help but just adore and love her. Her favorite flowers were daisies and carnations, the color of sky-blue pink, a color which she lovingly described as when the blue in the sky shares a shade of pink, and they blend as one. She had the most beautiful smile and the softest tone to her voice. I hung on her every word, smile, and touch. She hung the moon in my world.

My grandmother once shared a story of a time when she was living in a two-story flat, and a presence of a young boy with curly blond hair had come to the foot of her bed. He was giggling, and he said his name was Cuddles.

She mentioned this occurrence to a neighbor in the building who stated that "Cuddles" was the nickname of her little boy who had died a few years before from a tragic incident. My grandmother believed Cuddles wanted her to tell his mom that he was at peace and felt she was doing the Lord's work by doing so.

I knew then that I had a special gift that through my faith and love for God, I would always have a connection with my grandmothers and the spirits that continued to surround me; and to this day, I hold dear my grandmother's love of daisies and her favorite color "sky-blue pink."

My grandmothers and my faith in the Lord are what bring me through every storm in my life. So when I speak of premonitions and the many warnings or enlightenments in my life, you will understand that those connections are what guide me through every moment in my life and every life-altering decision that I make. My grandmothers are who molded me into the woman I am today, and they continue to play in my thoughts and carry me through the best and worst moments in my life.

Maybe you have not connected with spirits, had premonitions, or found a connection with God, but perhaps you have someone or many people in your life that you have connected with so deeply that you see them as a kindred spirit, a connection of the heart and mind that has you both riding the same wave of thoughts and feelings. Maybe there are fond memories of a loved one that keep you remembering words they had shared, and those words continue to guide you through your everyday life choices.

If you are ever so lucky to find amazing people in your life who carry these memories and feelings within you, hold onto them and cherish them. Life moves so fast, and we, while on this ride, sometimes forget to stop and smell the daisies, take notice of the beauty in a sky of blues and pinks, and appreciate what God has given us.

My life story really begins to bloom as a young girl of fifteen. I was always searching for who my first love would be, but I never really had much confidence in myself or my appearance and was almost certain I would never attract anyone. I believe the Lord always knew there was someone destined for me. I remember exactly where I was and the exact moment that I saw the young man who would not only be my first love but also my *forever* love. The minute this boy appeared in front of me, everything inside of me screamed, "He's the one!" I could not take my eyes off of him. He would subtly glance my way and flash me a sweet, lighthearted smile, and I would turn shyly away too nervous to look him directly in the eyes. That very day, I went home and wrote in my diary, "I am going to marry that boy."

It was a few days later when I was reading the horoscope section of the local newspaper and found my horoscope sign, Sagittarius, which read, "August 1988 will be a memorable one for you." I was not picking up the signs that were being given to me, but I realized later in life that those very signs were telling me about the soul mate I was destined to fall in love with during that exact month and year. Those feelings that were screaming from my soul were spot-on like the angels were whispering to my inner psyche, alerting me of what was to be.

This moment in my life would be my second childhood premonition. It would also be exactly what occurred. I first fell in love with that boy in August of 1988, and it was then that he asked me to be his girlfriend.

It was during our dating years that I learned the boy I loved was quite devoted to drinking alcohol and also partook in other addictive substances as well. It was not easy for me to accept this as I was taught in private school and church that this behavior was evil, and I despised it.

I continuously prayed that this would be a childhood phase and that I would be able to impress upon him a better way to be. I was wrong, at least for the first twenty years.

You can never prepare yourself for falling in love with someone who carries many inner demons, but as a young girl of faith, I hoped and prayed I could be his saving grace; and in many ways, he said I was.

There were a few other disappointments I endured as a teenager, not from my boyfriend but from my parents. My parents divorced a few weeks before I turned eighteen, and my mother did not handle this well.

Shortly after my parents' divorce, on Christmas Eve of 1991, the boy I loved asked me to be his wife. This was a delightful moment that I had to share with my grandmother. While showing off my ring to her, she told me he was a wonderful man, and he would take good care of me. She was not wrong.

At nineteen years old, a year and a half before I was to be married, I found myself feeling a strong sense that my grandmother would be leaving me soon and take her place in heaven, and I felt it was necessary to share with her how much I loved her and how very special she was to me in my life.

Shortly after talking with her, I would say goodbye to my grandmother with incredible heartache as the arms of the Lord reached down and carried her home.

Forever in my life when those colors of blue and pink take to the sky and the daisies come in bloom, I know my grandmother is there. Every place I have ever called home, I have found a bush full of daisies growing somewhere along the outside of the house, and it is then that I know that she has blessed my home. And for as long as I am living there, I know she is there with me.

On those occasions when she comes to me with warnings or words of wisdom, she comes through a field of daisies in my dreams and through the blazing blue and pink skies in my reality.

The reality for me now was that my mother had now lost her husband and her mother, two of the people she counted on the most, and I became the go-to person for my mother, the one she would always count on to care for her and to be the answer to all of her troubles.

This is when the good Lord threw a huge curveball my way, and I forgot to swing, letting that ball land right in my lap. I would now be accountable to answer not only to my soon-to-be husband's needs but also to my mother's needs. Suddenly my life was no longer mine; it belonged to both of them.

It took time before I realized this, and it didn't go well for me as years went on. Not long after my parents' divorce and shortly after getting engaged, I moved out on my own and in with my fiancé. This was when some of the greatest decisions in my life began to take place and when I was going to be counting on my grandmothers and my faith in the Lord the most.

Chapter 2

When things first started out with my fiancé and me living together, it was, of course, very exciting to be out on our own. We moved in together rather young. I was eighteen, and he was twenty. We had all the early-stage young couple arguments, money concerns, and house cleaning gripes, and how to handle my mother and her needs was always a discussion. What I was not expecting was finding myself sitting alone at night, waiting for my fiancé to come home from his all-night partying escapades.

Most of the time, his leaving was not agreeable; in fact, we fought quite often about it and how it affected me, waiting up all night hoping he made it home safely or wondering if he was still alive.

As a young girl, I was rather naive to the signs of addiction and pretty much assumed that anyone could just simply choose to stop consuming whatever it was if they really wanted to. I was also very new to addiction and how it affects the mind and the tricks that addicts will play in order to get away and do what they desire, but I was definitely learning firsthand.

It was not until finally, one night, I had enough and threatened to end our relationship through sobbing tears of frustration that my fiancé dropped the fight he was pursuing in order to leave. And in the guilt of seeing me so distraught, he admitted to me that he was an addict, and he had no control. Feeling defeated, he asked me to help him to be stronger. In my lack of knowledge on the subject and my want to love him and be there for him, I gave in and stayed.

He decided to really try to be better and reached out for help through Alcoholics Anonymous meetings. Wanting to take this journey with him, I joined the meetings for those living with loved ones suffering from addiction. It was not long before we both concluded that this would not work. In his meetings, they were exchanging numbers and hooking up with one another on the side; and in mine, they were telling me to run while I had no legal commitment to him. I adamantly disagreed with them, and he just simply refused to partake with his group.

We were managing fairly well on our own until one evening when my fiancé would come to me and share that we were invited to a friend's house for the weekend, and he wanted to go. I was not agreeable. I told him how unhappy I was spending time with this couple and begged him to stay home.

That night while sleeping, my grandmother came to me in a dream. And as I mentioned before, she walked through a field full of daisies toward my mother, and upon reaching her, my mother began to cry at that very moment I would see the flash of a lace veil swipe across my view and then suddenly wake up. This spiritual encounter was a warning from my grandmother that I would experience a brush with death.

I believed very much what she had shared with me, but at the same time, I could not convince my fiancé to stay home, and I was not willing to let him go without me. That night after arriving at our friend's house, I was not happy with my fiancé's behavior and wanted to go home early the next morning after very little sleep. What occurred next was the exact brush with death my grandmother warned me of.

I was driving home as my fiancé was much too inebriated to do so. While driving, I became very sleepy; and at some point, I drifted off to sleep behind the wheel of my car in the middle of a very large freeway. I was abruptly awakened when my car rear-ended a pickup truck on the freeway at which time I had slammed my face into the steering wheel and fractured my lower jawbone. My four lower front teeth were now laying on my tongue.

My fiancé was heartbroken and guilt-ridden over this, and after having my jaw wired, he did everything he could to take the best care of me. This was six months before we were to be married and what should have been a turning point in our relationship for the better, but not quite.

Six months later, we were married. I was a young wife of twenty years old, and we conceived our first child during our honeymoon.

It was not an easy pregnancy for me. During the first three months, I was very sick; and for my love, he was very frustrated and concerned for me. This, of course, was a good reason for him to drink, at least he thought so. The last seven months would be much easier. The nausea had dissipated, and the last two trimesters were going smoothly. We were so excited to see our sweet baby. Finally, the day had come, and we welcomed our first child, a beautiful baby boy, into the world.

For me, having a baby meant growing up fast and being a responsible, perfect mommy; for my husband, this meant, "Oh, hell. Life is about to get crazy. Time to drown my stress with drugs, alcohol, and rock and roll," or at least that was the way he felt.

Now do not misunderstand me. My husband was a great father, a hard worker, and the soul support for our new family, which he loved very much, but his ability to cope with stress and added responsibility was another ball game.

There were many late nights with high levels of intoxication for him and many sleepless nights for me. I would find myself getting more and more angry waiting up for him, and when I would hear the keys rattling in the door, I would climb into bed and pretend to be sleeping. I felt it was better to do this and prevent myself from lashing out and starting an argument, which I learned quickly was never a good idea with a drunken man. No, there was not any violence, just raised voices and a lot of hurtful words exchanged, nothing I cared to reenact.

Three years after our first baby was born, I became pregnant with our second child. This time, we were actually trying. We wanted our son to have a sibling, and after feeling so overwhelmingly blessed with our first child, we could not wait for our second to arrive and neither could he. He continuously tried to come early, and then after the doctor stopped my labor twice, my second son came late and was rather angry about it. The first vision of him was a screaming, shaking, red-faced, beautiful baby with much to say about his late arrival. Needless to say, we were in love.

Of course, with another addition to our family came more responsibility and more reasons for my husband to feel stressed and use his addictive nature to cope.

I am not going to sit here and tell you that my life was horrid and torturous and that I was forever miserable. I am actually going to share with you how I learned to handle what I was given in life because I loved someone enough to see it through even in the worst of times. (By the way, I am not and was not perfect myself.) My first steps to dealing with the curveball I was thrown were to fight, and fight I did.

After gaining weight from the pregnancies and essentially becoming someone different from the woman he first married, my husband started to lash out; and the really hurtful part was that he started to become distant from me.

With his love of music, he decided to start a band. He started out as the drummer and then quickly moved to vocals, which was a perfect spot for him. My man could sing!

At first, I thought this was a great idea, something to direct him to another source to relieve his stress, something more positive, except not so much. As much as he loved this, and I loved listening to him and seeing him light up, the band created an avenue for him to be in bars and added more nights of partying and even more time away from me.

In my frustration and heartbreak, I started trying to find ways for him to see me again. I started to appreciate flattery from other men, go to bars with friends, and spend money frivolously; and when this only worsened our relationship, I chose a different path and ventured into rebuilding myself.

I went back to school, became a medical assistant, and went to work in the medical field. I was continuously fighting with him, for him, and for us all at the same time.

I was getting angry and feeling more and more hurt. Here I was raising our boys, going back to school, working, fighting with bill collectors, and trying to appease a difficult mother, and he was out having the time of his life and making my life hell!

I was not just fighting against the partying and addictive consumption. I was fighting to get my husband back and to keep him alive, to keep our marriage strong, and to protect the sanctity of our home and the innocence of our children.

Through it all, the one thing we always agreed on was never to let the kids in on the craziness between us, and they were almost never aware until hiding it was not so easily done anymore.

Growing up in marriage is not an easy road. People change drastically as they continue to grow in life. Sometimes, the change is not what you are expecting, and you start to question if you should still be together or if you are still in love with the person they are now versus the person you fell in love with at the beginning.

I spent the greater part of my life with a man who I was head over heels in love with since the first time I laid eyes on him. I loved everything about him—his smile, his laugh, his sense of humor, and his immense passion for life, music, and our family. I always told him, "I love you and every part of you from the top of your head to the tip of your toes."

He was a man, a real man, who was never afraid to stand up for what he believed in and never backed down from a fight. He saw the greatness in all the little things that seemed to go unnoticed by almost everyone else. He had an incredible soul that looked beneath the layers within someone and saw the truly special pieces of someone else's soul. He was everyone's friend, adviser, and confidant.

He could make you feel like the only one in the room, the most beautiful blue eyes focused only on you, and with one gentle touch, he could set your entire insides on fire within seconds, at least mine. In the same token, he could make me rage with anger just as quickly. The worst part was he knew it.

He exuberated confidence, but deep down inside, he was wounded and filled with emotional anguish. He fought many inner demons as well as his own self-doubt. I tried hard to keep him uplifted and reminded him of what he did have in life and how special that was. He always agreed but just the same; he never stopped worrying and wanting more out of life. Deep down, it was wounding me too.

I hated to see him hurting or stressed, feeling like life was letting him down. I prayed for the Lord to help us find a peaceful life and happiness within our souls and with each other.

In search of this peace and happiness, we continued to work to support our family and, yes, to fight when the stress took him away into that seedy world that he ran to so often when things got tough. Our children were growing up, and the presence of our frustration with each other started to become apparent to them.

It is only a matter of time before the sweet little babies we brought into this crazy world start to grow up and become aware of their surroundings and the atmosphere around them.

As hard as you might try and as discreet as you might think you are being, children can sense the tension in the room, can hear the insensitive words being said, and can see the stern stares of disapproval and the looks of anguished and hurt.

Children are mystical, fascinating human beings. With a smile or a laugh, a gentle hug, or just the comfort of them in your arms, they can light up your world and make all of your worst feelings seem petty and small and just melt away. Our boys could always do this for us. However, I could not quite let go of the heartbreak I felt that they could feel, see, or hear any of what was occurring and have any emotions about it.

For my husband and me, it was never acceptable to allow your children to be raised in an unhappy environment or to receive any of the brunt of the frustration my husband and I were feeling toward each other and toward the world.

Marital strife is not uncommon, and in fact, it occurs in even the most perfect of marriages. Husbands and wives squabble over bills, money, personal frustrations, and sometimes just little things such as simply having a bad day; and you are now in a bad mood. The problem becomes when you add outside sources to the already-stressful things that occur with daily life and living; you get immense thunderstorms that even the music cannot drown out anymore.

Our boys were really good at blocking out the noise or at least pretending not to hear it. Until it was blasted in their direction, they never gave much inclination that they were affected.

Something I need to mention when I talk about our boys is that we were raising three beautiful boys; the two we brought into the world and our third little blessing, our sweet nephew, who spent most of his life growing up under our care and as part of our family. On the day he was born, mine was the first face he would see, mine were the first lips to kiss his cheek, and mine were the first words he would hear say, "I love you." He was without question our little boy too. Eventually, he and his little brother became permanent additions to our family. We will get to that story later.

Outside of all of our lives' own craziness and chaos and between each other, my husband and I believed ourselves to be a dynamic couple with extraordinary hearts, and we were always open and willing to take on the world together. No matter what our problems were or how big they might have been, we could see beyond them and know that we had responsibilities, and we were blessed to give more of ourselves to be there for others because we loved first.

Even with all of our downfalls, my revengeful acts, and his addictive behaviors, our boys were loved and well taken care of, spoiled really.

My husband's responsibility as the primary provider never faltered. He worked hard and rarely missed a day of work. He never let us down.

As a mom, I attended all of the boys' school activities, some with my husband alongside me, almost every game, school meeting, and event. I took my boys to every doctor and dentist appointment and managed all of the household upkeep and my duties as a wife. Together, my husband and I worked hard to give our children a normal and perfect life.

We made it a point to never let anyone see the deep dark behind-the-scene struggles we were going through. To us, those things were meant to be private and nothing we wanted to share with others. Of course, there were a few times when others were unexpectedly given a sneak peek of the troubles within. Emotions can be difficult to stifle sometimes, and as I mentioned before, addiction has a way of showing itself at the most inconvenient moments and bringing that sneaky person into play.

My husband sometimes relished the game of sneak. He said, "The sneaking out or away was the fun part" even though he felt horribly guilty and extremely remorseful the next day. The other reason for the sneaking away was to prevent the children from knowing and to make sure that I could not fight with him to stay home.

There were a few times I found myself left behind at people's homes or in venues where he had forgotten I was there with him, felt himself reacting to an urge, and just left to satisfy that need. Those were the interesting and, quite frankly, embarrassing nights for sure.

There was a time when the addictions started to really overcome my husband. He seemed constantly miserable and angry at the world and lashed out at everyone in it. It was during this time that I left our home and took our children with me, more than once. Each time, my husband knew how to charm me into coming home; it would help him that I loved him more than even he understood.

I knew I would never really leave him, not because I could not but because I did not want to. I knew he was meant for me and I for him, and it was my duty as a wife, who took very seriously her vows "in sickness and in health, until death do us part," to help him and to find a way to accept this curse he was burdened with and help him to beat it and find peace and happiness in his life.

Now before you go getting all gushy on me, I did not get to this realization as quickly as that. No, as I mentioned before, I lashed out—a lot! This girl was still fighting.

Chapter 3

On my journey to finding a way to accept and understand my husband as well as help him through his uncontrollable urges, I found myself quite angry, disgusted, and flat-out fed up. I felt unloved, unappreciated, and extremely disrespected. I knew he was not feeling much attraction to me anymore, and most days, I realized I was not the same ninety-pound girl he once fell in love with, and I had not put much effort into losing any weight or making any changes. But I had always tried to make myself look as attractive as I could, given the unforeseen circumstances of baby weight and added stress.

I always felt that if you loved someone, you loved them no matter what because love does not see flaws or faults, but this did not seem to be his mentality. I began to take notice that even though he was not interested or find me very attractive, many others were. I started to appreciate that flattery and feel good about it. To my husband, that meant I must have been going even further than just appreciating the flattering words; of course, that was not true. Nonetheless, he lashed out at me, and our marriage became a bit rockier.

In my struggle to make him see how he was making me feel about myself, I became even more frustrated and hurt. I realized he was never going to see how he played a role in all of this, and I gave up trying. I started going out to the bars with my friends. I was drinking, staying out late, and having a great time while at the same time feeling even more alone. Yes, I had my friends, but I was not with the one I truly wanted to be with—my husband. It was at this point that we started to lead separate lives.

To fill the void in my heart and to get back at my husband, I started going shopping and spending money on myself and the boys in extreme. I figured, if he could blow all kinds of our money on his addictions and his band, I could spend money on us. We elected to believe that our boys did not notice our behaviors, but they did.

The boys were growing up and were now aware of their dad's pathetic attempts to sneak off but were never awake to see his sickeningly inebriated self when he returned home. When they were awakened by his entrance late at night, they would become part of the pretending-to-be-asleep club that once only had one member—me.

They were also now starting to voice their own thoughts on the matter. This did not make life any easier and increasingly filled us both with guilt and heartache.

You see, living with someone who is burdened with addictions is not an easy road, and it does not just affect the addicted; it affects everyone who loves them and all who are a part of their life. The people closest to them, living within the same walls that they live in, are affected the greatest and are hurt the most.

One of the hardest parts to comprehend about this is that they are not intentionally aiming to hurt you. The most important part is gaining the understanding that they are riddled with anxiety, depression, and a deep-seeded pain that has brought them to this place in their lives and leaves them with great remorse and guilt for what they cannot control.

Until I was in nursing school and even after this, it was still a learning curve I had to adjust to and a surprising fact that you cannot just stop because you want to. Most times, addicts stop only because they have to, or they will die; and even then, that awareness is sometimes not enough to make them seek help to quit.

They must always be willing to seek help, and with this comes the need to gain the love, acceptance, and support of their loved ones. The first challenge is the addict wanting to seek help, wanting to quit, sticking with the fight to become sober, and finding the strength to maintain sobriety.

The second challenge is being willing to stand beside them and love them enough to carry the burden and fight through the trials and tribulations with them, to accept when they fail, and to give them the support they need to get back up and try again.

Trust me, it is one of the greatest challenges anyone can ever go through. The most difficult moment to swallow is when they stop trying or are never willing to make the attempt. Surprisingly, I have been through every one of these moments and survived them all.

We were always a great family; in fact, one of our boys mentioned one day while we were gathered around the dinner table, "My friends think we are a weird family because we are the only family out of all my friends that have dinner together every night."

In our boys' group of friends, we were a rarity because we not only sat as a family at dinner, but we were also still a full family with both mom and dad still married and under the same roof. We took pride in knowing this and how hard we strived to keep our family whole, not just for the betterment of our boys' lives but because we loved one another enough to see the worth in the fight to preserve our marriage.

My husband and I worked hard and fought plenty to keep our family strong and together, and amidst all of the trials we went through, we decided to refocus on our marriage and find new hope and renewed strength in our union as husband and wife, as lovers, as mom and dad, and as best friends; but are trials were not over yet. We always had my mother whose needs were aplenty, and now we had my sister.

As we were beginning to find some peace within our household again, not perfect, but much less strife than in the past, we were given a whole new focus to work through. This time, we would fight together as a family to make it through the challenges in front of us to get through one of the most important fights of our lives. This moment in our lives would turn out to be one of the greatest blessings we would ever receive after overcoming the climb.

Over the years and throughout all the struggles to beat the battles of addiction and bring down the devil's hand that was fighting against us, we watched our boys grow and become young men with quite opposite mentalities from one another and very different interests in life.

We had raised very strong-minded, determined, and talented boys with very boastful personalities. We had a very strong-bodied football player; a very dedicated and outgoing business-oriented leader; and a goal-oriented child, a swimmer, and an ROTC leader that had his sights set on the military, all with an amazing sense of humor and the greatest spirits imaginable.

My goal was to make sure that they held immense confidence and inner strength as men, were always respectful, remembered communication is always key, and steer clear of addiction and its demons. My husband's goal was to make sure they were prepared for the world ahead of them and the challenges life would throw at them.

Both goals would work hand in hand to carry them through their own paths in life. Our boys were capable of taking on a challenge and seeing their way through it without any irreparable damage to the path in front of them. As parents, we could not be prouder.

As individuals, we still needed some work. For my husband, work was wearing him thin, and he was tired of being a mechanic and wrenching his body out of sorts. He suffered from muscle pain, joint pain, and just plain exhaustion from the field he chose. He decided to provide me with an opportunity that would allow him a chance to find a way to break away from his career and choose a new path in life.

He encouraged me to seek my dreams, go back to school, and become a registered nurse.

I was elated that he would be willing to endure the time and effort this would take and the additional responsibility this would mean for him at home. While being willing to take this all on was quite admirable of him, and I very much appreciated him for doing so, it would serve as quite the challenge for him when it came to handling the stress and finding the strength to keep from resorting to his addictive nature for relief.

This, of course, would only mean that I too would need to be willing to endure a great deal of time and effort and to prepare myself for high-pressured strife as well.

He had a goal in mind, and he was going to make sure he achieved it.

I have always considered myself a strong woman, someone who could manage on her own if she had to, and with that thought in mind, I signed up for school.

You have to be accepted into nursing school, and shortly after signing up, I was accepted. The letter came in the mail right about the time a vital call that would change our lives, even more, came in.

A lady from the state department of health and human services was calling to ask my husband and me to assume temporary care of our two beautiful nephews as their home life was less than desirable. Of course, we agreed. This would be an increase in responsibilities in addition to me starting school and my husband already taking on additional chores at home; we would now be adding a three-year-old to the three teenage boys we were already raising.

With a great deal of excitement and a feeling of hope and happiness, I went back to school. Boy was it a stressful road. Of course, I enjoyed the friendships and the after-school drinks and study nights, but the pressure to succeed was unbearable, and my homelife was busy and exhausting.

After failing an exam and finding myself failing a class that would leave me having to wait until the following year to retake the class and continue on with schooling, I learned just how serious the pressure was. My husband made it abundantly clear that if I did not graduate with my nursing degree and relieve him of his primary provider role, he may quite possibly relinquish his responsibility through a divorce. It was not easy to work under that kind of pressure.

So I was working part-time, still being mom and wife and going to school with the mind frame that I could not fail and, on top of all of that, there were still some late nights for me, waiting for my husband to get home from a band night and all the involved activities that come with such an evening.

This is when our lives really started to get interesting. I was fighting to get through school, hold a job, and keep a marriage intact. He was managing the household but on full tilt, with surprises at every turn. We were both stressed, trying to work and manage our household as well as the added requirements of school and the family courts regarding our beautiful additions to our family. It was not much longer after this when we were called upon to add to our family, our third and fourth sons forever. What a blessing they were and have been in our lives; it's as if they have always been ours.

Things were definitely hectic for us; we seem to have very full plates, and trying to handle so much at once was starting to wear me thin. I finally broke. The emotion inside of me came out full throttle, and I suddenly just stopped fighting. Remember when I shared earlier my grandmother's words, "God will never give you anything you cannot handle?" Well, this is when I started questioning those very words and crying out to the Lord to step in and take over.

I had been racking up debt, trying to get through school and in some sort of revenge toward my husband and his behaviors, and only now after feeling so blessed with our sweet boys and the family we were did I feel as if I was letting everyone down. I needed to not only change the way I dealt with my husband's reactions to stress, but I also needed to change the way I dealt with my own.

It is amazing how much the good Lord believes you are capable of enduring. Even through all of our own struggles and failures, He still believed in us enough to add to our family and to know that our love was abundant enough to share it even more. He blessed us in having faith in us that we would be a strong, loving family, and nothing could ever break the foundation we built together.

One day, while my husband was at work, the children were at school, and I was home studying. I found myself feeling so helpless. I abruptly stopped what I was doing and hit the floor.

While down on my knees, I prayed, "Lord, I cannot do this on my own anymore. I need you now more than ever. I am sorry for my sins and my wrongdoings, and I am reaching out to you today, asking you to help me. Lord, I will do whatever you guide me to do if you will just step in and take over from here."

For the next five years, the Lord did just that!

It was after putting everything in God's hands that I realized I had to change my way of thinking. If I loved my husband, and I truly wanted to stay in this marriage, I needed to understand I could not change him, no matter how much anger I displayed, revenge I enacted, or hurt I inflicted. Only he could change him, and he had to want to change him. I just had to be willing to stay and be his inspiration for change, not his reason to run right into the fire.

I had to remind him what he had and how great life was even during the tough times. I had to stroke his ego and remind him how special he was, how loved he was, and how important he was to all of us. I had to help him seek what he loved, not what he was drawn to from stress, frustration, and uncontrollable urge. I had to know in my heart that I loved him enough to be this person for him and that he was worth that much to me to do so. This would be something I would have to remind myself of quite often.

I share a lot about my faith in the Lord, but I would be remiss to forget that the devil is still working his magic. There is a world out there where people go to make themselves feel invincible, where they are lured into a false pretense of believing that by participating in the wares slyly being passed their way, they can get away from their worries and slip into a lulling feeling of relief and release of all their stresses in life.

The devil comes in all forms, and he is only looking out for his own best interest. He is working with determination to prove to the Lord that he is more powerful and that his following will prevail over good. He comes into the darkness of your soul and plays with your mind as he works to persuade you to come to his side, and he instills in your psyche the idea that you are worthless and that your world is crumbling around you and that you will never climb your way out of the deep dark hole you feel you have fallen into.

This demon dangles in front of you false hope and a peaceful means to it all and convinces you that by indulging in his sweet methods of self-medication, you too can find happiness and sanctuary away from it all.

What is missing from all this luring and baiting is the reality that with this, you will eventually become the victim of a trap you cannot fight your way out of; and no matter how hard you fight, no matter how strong you think you are, you will find yourself losing the battle more often than not.

There were many times in the past that my husband would come home and share with me after a late night out that his heart felt like it was going to explode out of his chest, or there were moments while he was gone when he thought he was going to die. The substances that are consumed with addiction are damaging and can be deadly, depending on the level of consumption and the type of substance ingested.

I was no longer angry; I was afraid of the very thought that I could lose my husband to these horrible urges he could not deny.

The truth is, there are never easy answers or quick fixes that will take it all away. Life is hard but only if you choose to make it hard. Yes, you have the choice. You can look at your life and see the many blessings you hold, such as your life and your good health, the love of your loved ones and their good health, the home you have created, and the children you bore. You see, there are so many things we take for granted and choose not to see when we bury ourselves in negativity and personal pity and when we wallow in despair and wade in the dark waters of guilt and depression, anger and frustration, hopelessness, and greed.

Life is never easy, and I do not believe the good Lord intended it to be. We lost that grace when Adam and Eve ate the apple and had forsaken the Lord. If all of our choices were made based on the guidance of the Lord, we all could live a beautiful and simple life, one with grace and peace on this beautiful earth He has provided us.

We quite simply do not make all of our choices based on the guidance of the Lord but, instead, most assuredly make them based on our own emotions and desires.

Money, luxuries, and worldly desires are all nice; but a healthy mind, heart, and soul are absolutely vital. I was learning to understand this: to find acceptance in what I could not change and seek the guidance of the Lord for what I needed to do next.

Chapter 4

As a family, you would never know that we had any underlying issues at home. My husband and I always did our best to maintain a loving home and to give our children a perfect environment to grow up in. We loved our family and one another very much, and nothing was more important to us than that. My husband never let his behaviors affect his ability to financially support our family and be a great father.

For me, accepting my husband's addictive behaviors and learning that this was the life that the lord and chosen for me were a bit difficult to swallow, and I had no idea how he would guide me through it, but I was certainly going to need him to do just that.

As I said, the devil has no shame, and he thrives on showing himself. He is a proud spirit with a very deceitful nature that takes great joy in destroying your world. I had no plans to let him destroy mine. There was still a fight left in me, but this time, I was not fighting my husband or his addictions. I was fighting to find ways to prevent him from ever seeking those addictions again. This was a battle I would never give up on.

I wanted to prove that we, as a couple, were stronger than the evils bestowed upon us and that together, we could face any challenge and overcome it. This would begin with me rebuilding myself. I faced the stress of school and the threat of defeat, and I continued on. I started swinging at the fastballs and daring the curveballs to come my way. I was ready!

I began drowning out the worries over the addictive behaviors of my husband and denying the devil's plea to see me give up and fall in defeat. I took on a new view of our lives and began to carve out a brighter path in our world with a goal to win, to survive the odds, and to become champions of our own destination. This would not come without my husband's willingness to cover the grounds while I pursued the enemy and burrowed through the trenches to reach the light ahead.

There were days when the weakness set in, and the hopelessness darkened my path. I got lost in self-pity and cried out, "What about me? Who is caring for me? Why am I responsible for his needs, the children's needs, my mother's needs, and no one is responsible for mine? Why does no one seem to care how I feel? Why must I continue to be strong and fight this alone? When does life start to be about my happiness?"

Our life together was somewhat of a roller coaster all the way through. We never stopped having to struggle, and it seemed we were never destined for breaks. We were a team of fighters, but we also became a team that entertained the idea of quite possibly giving up. I myself started to lose faith in God and believed He had just walked out on me and left me to fend for myself while placing me in a life that seemed nothing but frustrating and hard. My husband was losing faith as well and believed that God had let him down. Our anger at God did not serve us well.

You see, when you step away from your faith and stop listening to God, you lose all hope that you can carry on. Your anger becomes so fueled that you make bad decisions to try to fix the choices you already made that did not work out so well. You denied the one direction you could turn to and the one source you could give all your troubles to and took away the option to allow God to take over.

There were two sources in my life I knew I could talk to, who would always be there to listen, my grandmother and the Lord. I dismissed them both. I was angry. I hated the world. I felt letdown and like everything was hopeless. I never felt so alone in all of my life, and the choices I was making were only setting the world on fire at home.

I was not getting through to my husband, but instead, I was giving him reason to resent me. This was not working the way I wanted it to. So I gave up. I stopped fighting, and I walked away, not from my husband or our home but from the anger and the attempts to make him notice me and change himself.

It seemed the only way I found strength was through the Lord, and the only way I was reminded to love unconditionally and respect myself no matter what was through my grandmother. I needed them in my life, and I needed to remind my husband that he needed the Lord too. I told him, "The Lord helps those who help themselves." We were not helping ourselves, our children, or each other.

I began to realize that I needed to choose my happiness and the destination I wanted in life. I worked tirelessly to get through school while continuing to fight the almost daily battles that were coming full force and nonstop toward me. I reminded my husband that his success relied on my success, and the need for his best behavior was necessary in order for me to focus and achieve my associate's degree as a nurse. My husband proved that he could rise to the challenge and be the man I needed him to be.

After two long years of constant studying and striving to rise above the difficult moments, I walked that stage and collected my associate's degree. The first punch at the devil landed dead center. I kept my vow to the Lord, and I did what He was guiding me to do. I took care of my children, I loved my husband, and I cared for my mother. And through it all, I found new strength in myself along the way.

I gave up the need to seek vengeance against my husband's behaviors, and I stepped away from the nightlife. I stopped spending money, and I cut up my credit cards, made my payments, and eventually my debt was gone. I knew then the good Lord had seen my efforts and guided me through. I was creating a new me, a better me, a faithful me and directing a new pathway for all of us. I could feel the spirit of the Lord within me and new happiness in my soul.

I no longer felt hatred toward my husband or myself. I was healing from within through my faith in the Lord, in myself, our marriage, and our family.

Life was feeling good, and it was now my husband's turn to feel the benefits and take leave from his position as a mechanic; however, the devil does not go down easy. He rises to a challenge, and he finds new ways to tear you down. He and my husband were still giving me a run for my money.

I was under the impression that if I completed school and successfully achieved my degree, giving him the ability to retire at forty-five years old would relieve the stress and at very least get him to decrease his need for the addictive devices he would seek, but I was wrong. Not completely wrong, he did mellow out for a while, and the smile that came with watching him wave goodbye to his dreadful job was definitely rewarding. I was proud to have placed myself in a position to allow him the possibility for the opportunity he always dreamed of having—a brewery.

I was still working on my acceptance of what I could not change and figuring out what I could do to preserve our marriage and keep him focused on the positive and deterred from the negative. We spent many evenings talking about his dreams for a brewery, our dreams for happiness, and prosperous retirement.

The thing is, no matter how much love you have for someone or how much the two of you have achieved in life, for some, it is just never enough.

As much as you might believe you have it all figured out, you really never do. While you are sitting behind the wheel, happily content with the life you have and driving along as if everything is perfect, and nothing could possibly jump in your way, with addicts, the risk is always there.

It is just a matter of time before you become so comfortable with the road you are on that you let your guard down for just a second, and then BOOM! You flinched, and the devil jumped in your way again. Suddenly, you find your husband backing down the driveway and back to the late nights again. After a while, you get tired of being on high alert, and you just blow out the candle, lay down your guns, and go to bed, hoping when you wake up, he is there safe and sound and each time finding the courage and determination to battle on.

When I talk about acceptance, it is not really the acceptance of what the addict is doing or even the behaviors involved; it is really the acceptance that there is not anything you can do or say that will ever stop the addict or take away the demons deep within their soul.

No matter how much you try, until the addict hits rock bottom and is ready to quit on their own, you are powerless.

You just need to decide, Do you love the person enough to stay with them and continue to remind them they are loved and to pray that the Lord keeps them safe and brings them home alive every time they leave?

For me, praying and having the Lord by my side was really what kept me grounded and staying strong for myself, my children, and my husband. Having faith in the Lord was what allowed me the sanity to get through the late nights and the worry and gave me the ability to manage my home all the while. For us, communication was the strongest key to our marriage and the many trials and tribulations we endured throughout it. No matter how uncomfortable the conversation may have been, we felt it vital to share the good, the bad, and the ugly we felt about each other or our circumstances in order to move on and continue with a happy marriage.

Trust me, I never stopped telling him how much this was hurting me and how scared I was for him and us, and I never stopped reminding him just how special his life and our lives were and of all the blessings we already had in life. Of course, he never stopped telling me how unsatisfied he was and how much more he wanted from me and from life. There were times when I questioned whether he still loved me and if I was enough for him, and he always seemed to have a way of making me believe that I was being silly, and there was no question of his love for me.

In all reality, I was blaming myself for his feelings of unhappiness because I could not take away all of his constant obsession to worry, and I so wanted to.

There were times when neither one of us could seem to put a finger on the problem and correct it, and we, instead, just lashed out at each other and pointed fingers and spewed hurtful words and evil-eyed daggers at each other. We talked about separating and finding our own happiness without each other, but we were never able to follow that through. Our love for each other just would not allow it.

I cannot tell you that everyone can fight through these battles and come out more in love for it or even willingly stick around to see if the promised land is there at the end. The life of living with some-one with addictions is not for the faint at heart and typically is not something that most are willing to endure. I can tell you that we are guided in our lives by a God that is so magnificent that if you allow Him to lead you in the life he has chosen for you, you will find the glory in the fight along the way. You will feel fulfilled and rewarded, and you will find yourself in a life that is just and worth every bit of the wait.

As I said before, I had to continue to remind myself that the good Lord had a reason for everything that was happening in my life and that if I stood strong and dredged through the difficult times, I would learn why He needed me to go through them; and I knew I would cherish the beauty I would find in the end as my reward for showing strength and endurance through it all, at least I hoped.

Addiction is like a light switch. Every day, you go through the motions of flipping the switch to turn on the light with hopes that it will shine, never really knowing when the day will come when you go to flip that switch and pow, the light blows out, and you are left in complete darkness with no light shining through. So with every burned-out light, you replace it with a new one and start over again, flipping the switch one day at a time. My point is, you go through every day hoping that the day will go smooth with no challenges, and it is like Russian roulette. You never know when the urge is coming, and they are suddenly gone, without a warning; they sneak off to satisfy their urge. I am not sure you ever really get comfortable with this. You just do the best you can to have faith and trust in the Lord to keep them safe.

I believe the Lord placed me in my husband's life because He believed I was strong enough to be the person he needed to see him through his personal struggles and help him battle the beast of addiction.

In my heart, I know no one loved him more than I did, and no one wanted the best for him more than I did, and no one tried harder to get him through it all than I did. In the end, the addict has to want it for themselves because no matter how much you love them or how much you want better for them, without them truly wanting to find sobriety, it will not happen.

A powerful lesson I learned after twenty-six years of trying to fix it all and hoping for change is that it does not change because you want it to.

I have never been someone who gave up easily or went down without a fight. I stood by my husband, and I defended him to the world. I could see the greatness in him, the heart, the sweetness, and the lost soul; and I was not going to let him go through this alone.

I made the choice when I married him. I knew who he was and the burdens he carried, and I chose him anyway. I was committed to my vows. I had children with him, and I now had to stand strong and brace myself for the tough days and be there for my children during the rough times.

I do not believe in divorce, and I believe in the power of being a family and children having their father and mother in their lives while growing up. A very gentle soul reminded me how important it is to allow your children to be children and enjoy their childhood without all the duress of a husband and a wife's messes. Our children should not have to pay for our problems. We are responsible for their lives; they are not responsible for ours.

Yes, women are strong; and of course, we can manage to play both roles. But who is this better for you? The children? I know sometimes you have little choice, and you must always consider the safety and well-being of you and your children, but think hard. Do not make this an easy decision. Do not just throw your hands up and walk away. Remember, the addict did not choose this either, and they desperately need the people they love to be there for them; otherwise, all hope is lost for them.

Does this mean if, given the choice, I would be with someone with these burdens? No. If I had known what I was up for, I may have walked away before getting involved, but you cannot help who you fall in love with, and you cannot sway the Lord's purpose for you.

Today, I am learning that the choice I made to stay and go through the struggles may not have been the wisest choice, and my children did not always agree with me; but for me, it was the only choice. No matter the frustration they felt with their dad, they loved him so much and learned so much from him through all the ups and downs; and his presence, while not perfect, was vital to their growth and the amazing men they are today.

As women, we can preach to our children what a great man is to us and how they should carry themselves as men, but having their dad in their life allows them to learn by example and also to learn from his mistakes as well as yours. For a daughter, it allows her to see the kind of man she aspires to be with and what not to accept from a man as well.

We must always consider the consequences of our actions, take the time to step back, take a breath, and look around us and remember that we are not in this alone. Your decisions are not just about you and your desires; they include so many and so much more. Consider who you may be hurting before you step out and make a choice that may suddenly see your whole world crumble, and you have no way of taking it all back.

Acceptance is not the act of giving in or giving up; it is the willingness to take on the challenge, tie back your hair, roll up your sleeves, and wade through the trenches. Climb up the hills, fight back the tears, and stay steadfast in the fight of your life! Can you do it? Are your life and the well-being of your family worth it? Do you have what it takes deep inside of you to fight this battle? Do you love your addict enough to fight alongside them and destroy their demons with them? If you answered yes to any or all of these questions, hold on. It is going to be a nasty ride but worth every mile.

The challenge starts with knowing what you are up against and finding the best way to get through it. Most of the time, you will find yourself feeling helpless as you are watching it happen, and you can do nothing to stop it. You must find the strength within you and the love you feel for your loved ones to remind them how valued they are and that you are here for them no matter what. You need to have the compassion to reach out your hand and say, "I will help you up, lift you up, and hold onto you until you are steady on your feet. I will love you through it all. I am here for you, for us, and for our family."

When you find yourself in love with someone who is fighting addiction, know that the Lord is giving you a challenge and looking to see what kind of fight you have in you and just how well you will handle the battle.

How much faith do you have? Do you believe the Lord will never let you fall? Do you believe He is walking with you through it all? I do.

I believe in you, I believe in the Lord, and I believe in me. There is nothing that cannot be achieved if you wield your sword through the Lord.

So who is caring for me? Who is responsible for my needs? Who is caring about my feelings? Well, that is the simplest of answers—I am. I must care and be responsible for myself, and no one is intentionally neglecting my feelings. They just have not learned to see past their own.

My husband never stopped loving me and taking care of me when I needed him most. He just wasn't very good at taking care of himself. With the Lord by my side, there is always someone other than myself, loving me. He is gracious and loving and all-forgiving, and I am forever blessed.

I accept the things I cannot change; I accept the life I have been given and the challenges I must face because I know I will never face them alone.

It is never easy in a relationship to tell someone you love that they are hurting you or to know that they are hurting themselves, and there is very little you can do to help them or stop it from happening. My life has been an incredibly interesting journey.

This is the importance of holding onto your faith. No matter how difficult it may seem and how letdown you may feel, never let go of your faith; and always remember that the Lord is not letting you down. He is merely seeing how strong you really are. He is testing your trust in Him.

I am a firm believer that God has a plan for each and every one of us, and we may not like the road we are on or the life we are living at the moment, but there is a purpose for it; and if we open our hearts and listen, God will carry us through. The path we are on is also guided by our own hearts and the choices we make.

God is watching, and He is waiting for you to realize that you need Him, so He will let you make the effort to push yourself up, strengthen your wobbly legs, and carry yourself through life until you find yourself losing control and heading toward the ground. And then when you are at your last attempt to maintain your stance, He will grab hold of you and renew your strength to go on if you reach for Him.

There will be times when you refuse to reach, and you insist you have this. When He knows you have given it your all, and you have completed the task at hand, this is the time when He will reach down and surround you with His love and strength and see you through even though you never asked.

These moments do not happen often, but you will know when they do. He is always watching and waiting for you to seek Him and need Him and to know that life is greater when He is present in it.

I pray that you will find that, if you have not already. I hope that everyone finds it. Our world certainly could use a little more focus on the Lord and a lot less focus on ourselves.

Chapter 5

Sometimes, it takes reaching your last straw to finally see that you must make changes, or things will only get worse. We made the decision to search for a new home and a new environment. This plan did not go over well with our children. Three of our boys were older and not so enthused with the idea of moving away from their friends and the home they knew. One of our boys was planning to attend college in lower Michigan the next fall and was not at all happy that we might be moving away from him.

Another boy was getting ready for his senior year of high school, and the idea of spending his final year of school and graduating without his friends seemed less than ideal for him. Our oldest would need to find a place to live as he had been living with us at the time, and this just broke my heart. I knew the focus was to get us away from the old and the temptations surrounding us so that we could find happiness within ourselves and each other again. The focus was on keeping our family whole.

We both knew this, and so we stayed steadfast with our plan and continued to search for the best place for all of us. Sometimes the hardest decisions are the ones that are the most worthwhile. Sometimes the toughest battles make you the strongest.

Our battles were not over yet. Oh, no, we were just finding a new place to continue the fight and hoping we would come out with renewed purpose and love for each other. We wanted to rebuild our friendship, strengthen our marriage, and reaffirm the foundation we had built for our family.

We needed a renewed purpose, a change of scenery, and a new start in both our lives and our marriage. Nothing is more difficult than the realization that the people you love and those who are part of your daily lives are having a negative impact on your life. Nothing is more awakening than determining that in order to find happiness and save your marriage and your life, you must leave everyone else behind.

You must choose God's direction and free your mind and soul from everything in your past. It was a great feeling to know that our love was more important to us than anything else in the entire world, and it was worth fighting for and sacrificing everyone else for. The one person we took along for the ride, outside of our immediate family, was my mother.

This was going to be interesting.

The first step in all of this was finding the right place to call home. We had two places in mind: Wisconsin and Upper Michigan. Ultimately, we made both our home. Our first choice was Upper Michigan, and when I say Upper Michigan, I am talking almost all the way to the tip, the farthest north, shy of copper harbor you can go, Allouez. Literally the last building you see displays the words "Welcome to the last place on earth." This was going to be an adventure. Loading everything up, our stuff and my mother's, was a challenge in itself.

One of the greatest reasons we chose Upper Michigan was because my husband's mother and sister live there, and we felt it would be ideal to have our family together and be able to take care of both his mother and mine. Did I mention my husband does not handle stress well? My husband believed all would be okay for him because he would not be working. As I shared with you previously, he retired from his previous position, and now I was going to support our family while he cared for our mothers. Oh, boy!

I found a position as a nurse rather quickly and started my career with a less-than-positive bang. The nurses' pay in Upper Michigan is quite a bit less than anywhere else and not what we had in mind. Relinquishing things to the mentality that we would need less in the

UP and that we had paid for our new home outright and would not have a house payment, we decided we would make it work.

I was hired to work for the new doctor who was being hired, and I was certainly excited to start fresh with someone who was also starting fresh with the company. I figured we could learn together and create a great working relationship based on sharing the same challenges. I could not have been more blessed to work with such a wonderful man. We meshed perfectly together and carried each other through the storms. We shared the same concerns and built quite a friendship together. The staff we had and the original provider who was already a staple there were also terrific, and between both providers and our staff, we made that place a joy to come to and a pleasant place that did not feel much like work most days.

It was then I knew that being the sole provider for my family was going to be a breeze.

Homelife was a different story. It started out wonderful. Everyone was happy. My mother was overjoyed to be living with us, my husband was ecstatic to be retired, and our youngest son was fitting in beautifully at school. My mother-in-law was beyond thrilled to have us all together and living so close to her, and it seemed we were going to be very happy with our new environment.

Everything was going perfectly until it wasn't.

My husband had been dreaming of starting his own brewery and being his own boss of something that he really enjoyed. He was busily working to put together a business plan and searching for the perfect building to start his dream. This would not be an easy process and one that led to a few letdowns and a lot of anger and agitation for him. The business plan was the easy part for him. My husband has a brilliant mind and an amazing knack for organized detail and perseverance. He already had many all-grain brew recipes and a well-thought-out idea of what he wanted. It was just not so easily done in such a limited area. Finding a building to get all this started would prove to be a feat in itself and one he would never seem to accomplish.

My mother was happily enjoying her new room and her beautiful bed that came with the move as well as being with all of us. She was overjoyed that she would not be alone anymore and that she would now have all of us surrounding her daily. My youngest son was making new friends every day, and my senior in high school was making the best of being the new guy at school. I was excited to get up every day and go to a job I loved and work among people who made me smile every day. It seemed we had found a perfect place or was it a perfect storm?

The one thing I forgot to mention in Upper Michigan, with all its beauty and peacefulness, is that there are bars on almost every corner. My husband planned to visit all of them to see how they ran things and get ideas for his business in the works. Suddenly, I was nervous. My heart was doing somersaults, and my mind was racing with the *oh-no*s and the *what-if*s. I knew he had all this time on his hands and no one to keep him home since I was working.

He spent many days helping his own mother with the upkeep of their family home and her household repair needs, which gave him a great sense of pride and a rewarding feeling, knowing he could be there to help and take care of her. Meanwhile, my mother was getting bored and feeling like she was just stuck in another house, while we were gone all day. She was envious that I could leave the house every day and be around people and started to feel as if she was alone all over again. Life at home was starting to spiral out of control.

Once again, I was trying to keep everything peaceful and reminding everyone that we needed to work together and to be on the same page with one another. I was setting the stage for why we made this move and what our end goals were and instilling the need to keep things civil and to be in control of ourselves.

I was diligently trying to be my husband's cheerleader, my mother's confidant and counselor, and of course the go-to person for the boys' needs.

My husband, being a man of organized behaviors or obsessive-compulsive disorder, did not fare well with my mother's far-from-organized thoughts or behaviors. My mother, being a nervous person with much always on her mind, would unintentionally leave small messes behind because her reactions moved faster than her thoughts; and my husband, with very little patience and a short temper, did not handle this well.

I was busy working and coming home to be the go-between trying to gently advise my mother to pay better attention to her behaviors at home while trying to persuade my husband to be more understanding and a little less uptight.

Now I was everyone's enemy, and the attack was on. Both my mother and my husband are similar creatures. They seem to have out-of-nowhere mood swings, dual personalities if you will. Neither of them wanted to take any fault and/or believe that they were creating any of the chaos that seemed to be occurring on a daily basis. Instead, they were blaming each other for their frustrations and anguish.

I tried instilling accolades to both of them when days went well, and I even started trying to help my husband find a building for his brewery to give him some inspiration and hope for better days ahead, but to no avail. The bitterness ensued, and the resentment toward each other and myself grew.

What does my husband do when he is stressed? He turns to his addictive nature, and so he did—with full force! The environment at home was ugly. I was resenting my mother for being there and stirring the pot. My mother and my husband were resenting everyone, and my kids were frustrated and some nights worried about what might be coming when dad arrived home. Yes, he was pulling late nights again and coming home as someone none of us recognized and no one wanted around.

Pretending to be asleep was not working anymore because he would come in and be so obnoxious that he would wake me up, and I would have to leave the room in order to get any peace. It seemed I had now found hell. The devil was putting all of his chips in and giving it his all to send us right over the edge, and it was working. One morning, in a fit of anger over my frustration with him, my husband packed up and said I could have the house. He was leaving. It was over, and sadly, I was happy to hear it.

I just wanted some peace for my boys and myself, and I was tired of being the doormat for everyone. The next step was finding my mother a place of her own and learning to live on my own.

That decision did not even last twenty-four hours. It barely lasted my full workday before my husband was calling me to talk about our situation and how we needed to change it. He stated that he loved me too much to be away from me and that he wanted to come up with a plan to get back on the right track and find our happiness again. The first step in his plan was to find Mom a place of her own. The second step was to move again.

Our initial plan was to take a weekend trip on our own and rekindle what we were starting to lose. We chose Green Bay as our vacation spot, and we had a wonderful time. Our love was greater than even we realized. Our feelings for each other never missed a beat, and now we had found a new place to call home. Next, we had to start laying out a full plan and finding a place to move to as well as new employment for me. Surprisingly, even he was deciding to go back to work, temporarily of course.

The biggest discussion, one he did not wish to entertain, was being in control of his behaviors and losing the whiskey drinking for starters. I decided I would not push the issue but rather trust that with our plans in place, he would be happier and slow down on his own.

We found my mother a temporary apartment. She was not at all impressed and put up quite a fight about it, but this would just be until we had all of our moving plans in perspective. This was a great beginning, but it did not have the impact I expected on my husband's drinking and frequency at the bars, and he was still coming home a nightmare. This behavior continued well into our move to Wisconsin before I reached my peak of frustration and flew completely off the handle.

My husband was angry at the world and tired of being letdown. He was fighting with his mother, my mother, me, and himself; and he never felt like he was winning. The Lord was challenging him, and the devil was enticing him; unfortunately for all of us, the devil was winning. I was at the other end of that spectrum, trying to hold on to the person I loved, trying to make him see himself in both lights, and convincing him to find the worthwhile in life again and be the better guy that I loved and adored.

I found a nursing position in Wisconsin, and he found a job as well, and we started the moving process again. We were sure tired of moving and all of the challenges that came with it, but we knew that our search was not done. We had not quite found our happy place yet, and this was a definite necessity before our marriage was lost forever.

Our search for a new place to live led us to a temporary apartment that would house us until we found our new home in Wisconsin. Of course, we would find a new apartment for my mother as well, and the new move was on. We were headed to Wisconsin to start over again.

No, the battling was not over, but it was certainly getting closer to the end.

Chapter 6

Every struggle in life is not a battle between one another but rather a fight against the odds, the indifferences, the challenges thrown at you by the world around you, and the devil himself. For some of us, the battles seem to never end. Everyone gets beaten down with financial woes and some form of heartache in our lives, and each one of us has our own way of making it through these struggles or at least finding ways to make it easier to bear the frustrations life throws at us. There are, of course, times when the frustrations just seem unbearable, and we feel like we will never beat the odds and find our peace and happiness in life.

For my husband and me, it seemed hopeless more often than not. We did not have anyone leaving us inheritance or family throwing money our way. Most of our family, well really all of our family, are middle-class Americans or outright poor. Of course, our battles were not just financial but just rotten luck, and we were always finding ourselves fighting in the trenches to carry our shield of honor, loyalty, hope, and love. Life never seemed to stop throwing wrenches in our path to victory.

The one certainty I always had in my life was my connection with my grandmother and her special way of coming to me to heed warnings and enlighten me to happiness on the horizon. Her subtle moments of reminding me she is there have walked me through many trials and tribulations in my life. Every time I see a beautiful sunset with a hint of pink in the blue sky, I know she is telling me, that everything is good and will be well tomorrow; and every time I see a daisy in my path, it brings a smile to my face, knowing she is following alongside me and clearing a perfect path for me so that I will not find danger or pain along the way. There are even moments when I can smell so strongly the Coty powder she used to wear, and I know she is most certainly with me then.

When I am at my lowest point and giving up hope, she reminds me to seek the Lord and to remember He will see me through my difficult moments if I will choose to lean on Him. Her warnings never come lightly but always seem to be meant to prevent me from taking the wrong path, like the car accident that occurred earlier in my life.

I cannot begin to explain why, but I believe that I have a connection with God that goes without measure. I am blessed and cursed to be given warnings when someone dear to me is going to rise to the heavens and take their place with Him. I see these messages in dreams and even sometimes in reality.

Once I was in the bathroom, getting ready for the day, my shower curtain blew upward as if a wind had come through; but the window was not open, and there was truly not a lick of wind. Minutes later, my mother called to tell me that my cousin had passed on. There are times when a family member who has passed will come to me in a dream with a message for a loved one that only they can understand, and after sharing with them, their hearts are touched; and they believe in what I am sharing because only they know what those words mean. I do not have any real answers for these spiritual enlightenments that happen to me, except to say that the Lord must have a reason.

It is when these warnings come to me and are about me that I sometimes miss the message or catch on a little too late. Not all warnings or messages directed toward my life are missed, and some come with enlightenment and assurance that I am doing as I should and that the choices I am making are the right ones. My husband always seemed a bit freaked out by these things and usually asked that I not share if something bad was going to happen. He preferred to just take it as it came. I preferred to take the message and try to prevent the bad from coming our way. I did not always beat the storm that was rolling in.

When those storms come in, I find myself standing in the middle of them with the winds blowing incessantly, the rain smacking me in the face, and the hail stinging my skin. In the midst of it, I am screaming at the top of my lungs, "Stop it! God help me! Why does it hurt so bad? How is this fair? When will this storm be over?"

All the while I am fighting. My arms are swinging, and I am trudging through the flooded waters, pushing through the violent winds and enduring the stinging of the hail, trying to find the sun shining across a sea of sky-blue pink, searching for the soft field of daisies to lay my exhausted body down to rest and find peace, and listening for His voice to tell me, "It is all going to be okay. I've got you."

Most times He does, and then there are times when there is no response, no spiritual answer. And I remain steadfast holding on and awaiting the moment when He says, "It is over, child. Continue on." He does not always provide these answers, but I know within me that I have endured the storm and survived the challenge, and I am strong enough to carry on.

One of my favorite Bible verses is Philippians 4:13, "I can do all things through Christ who strengthens me." I carry this within my heart and soul to remind me that through Him, my strength is unwavering. I have shared this with my husband in hopes that he, too, would find his strength in the Lord and not in the bottle or any other addictive vice.

My great-grandmother shared with me once the shortest verse in the Bible. John 11:35, "Jesus wept."

She said, "Jesus weeps because He cannot save us all. We must seek our own salvation through Him, and with His guidance and assurance, He will someday carry us home to the land of promise and peace." It goes without saying that you may find yourself seeking salvation more than once. I know I have, but I will never lose faith that He is there beside me even when it feels as if I am all alone.

There was one such moment when I was not sure the Lord was there, and I begged Him to take control. I felt the need to remind Him how much I had placed in His control and how it was vital that He not let our family down now.

Our second oldest son had become very sick and ended up in the hospital. He was diagnosed with Graves' disease and type 1 diabetes. He was down to 138 pounds at six feet. He was extremely fatigued, and his body was shutting down from an overactive thyroid.

I had taken a phone call from him one morning, informing me that he was being admitted to the hospital and was awaiting answers as to what was happening to him. It was a few hours later when he would call me crying to alert me that the hospitalist on staff had advised that if he had family, they should come. Of course, I was on the next plane.

After giving God a good stern talking, I arrived at my son's bedside and learned that they were able to get his blood sugar and thyroid levels under control, and he was going to be okay. This would be a very large turning point in our lives and one that we would never forget. I am forever grateful to God for hearing my cries and answering so greatly even after I had been so angry toward Him.

We made it through the initial storm, and we came out only slightly scathed. We needed to find a home, move from our apartment, and ensure a stable environment for our youngest son. It did not take long before we found that perfect place to call home, and life started to seem brighter for all of us. I had changed places of employment a few times, and to this day, I am still seeking the place that I am meant to be in my career.

I believe this book is my beginning to a new path for me, one with bright promise and feelings of reward for what I love. I love to help others; I love to shine a light on what others miss seeing and give them hope and reassurance that life can be better and that someone out there does care and believes that they do matter. I want to provide understanding and comfort in people's lives. I want to share the blessings of the Lord and how he can be your best strength, and you can find your greatest security through Him.

Yes, we made it through another storm, perhaps one of the strongest but certainly not as great as the one I would endure next. This could quite possibly be my life's impossible storm.

We were finally on a positive path to victory. My husband had found his control against his addictions after a well-battled storm together and we had found our friendship and happiness together again. My best friend was back, and I was a very happy girl. We were no longer battling each other; we were now battling the tough moments together and beating them one by one.

We found that we were happiest together when we were working on the same page, and through this, our blessings had started to take place.

Our finances were getting better. We paid off some debt, and we were seeing positive outcomes for our hard work. We even won a small jackpot at the local casino.

My husband has always believed in God even when he felt letdown by Him. He just seemed to have a tough time learning to let go and let God take over for him. It seemed now that he was slowly turning things over to the Lord and learning to enjoy the life he had.

We were setting up our new home and enjoying the happiness we felt to have it. We were learning to have fun together and enjoy each other again. We were learning to be partners as well as friends. Our relationship was stronger than ever. There were small moments of relapse but nothing so major that we could not endure it and move on. After all, we had been through far greater trials in the past.

We began to start planning our retirement and where we wanted to be when this occurred. We were searching for lakefront property and dream building what we would be enjoying when this time came. Our boys were succeeding beyond our wildest dreams.

Our oldest became licensed as a mortgage lender, and our second oldest graduated from a university with a bachelor's degree in business. Our third oldest graduated from college and the police academy with an associate degree, and our youngest was enjoying his new home and friends and achieving excellence in his new school. Life was good!

We were both working. I found a position close to home, and it seemed we had officially beat the odds and came to the end of the trenches we were always trudging through. God was truly blessing our hard work.

We started every day with a good morning kiss and a smile and sent each other off to work with an, "I love you," and, "Have a great day, babe." We would text each other throughout the day and remind each other to stay positive and how much we loved each other. We came home with hugs to give and receive and shared stories from our day. We counseled each other through the tough days and were cheerleaders for each other on the best days.

I told my husband I was the happiest girl in the world. I finally had everything I had ever dreamed of and more. He was beyond happy to hear this and felt very proud that he no longer felt the devil's grip on his soul.

Have you ever had one of those moments where you suddenly say to yourself, *This is too good to be true. Things are too perfect. Can life truly be this perfect and last forever?* Well, I did. Of course, I shrugged it off as my own silly insecurity, and then the pandemic came. We were put on leave from work, and everyone was mandated to stay home and stay safe. We were all required to mask up, and my husband was starting to feel a bit claustrophobic and extremely irritable from it all. When you lose the freedom to enjoy the outdoors, you start to find ways to enjoy the indoors; and when boredom sets in, your mind starts to work overtime. You become agitated and frustrated, and then the urges start to work their way in.

We made every effort to make the best of a less-than-perfect situation. We built puzzles, we watched movies, we played games, we listened to music, and some of us drank. Now it wasn't too bad at first. We actually even had a few beers together while listening to music and building puzzles. We were still teammates and enduring the battle together. The months would drag on while we waited out the pandemic demands, and it was not looking good for me and my new position at work.

I would find out after many months that they would not be keeping my position, and I was being let go. I did, however, have a bit of luck on my side. I had already applied to a new position just in case this should occur, and they had called me for an interview just before my notice was given at my previous position. All of this chaos had my husband stressed, and that is never a good thing. I successfully got the job, and the tension started to lighten up just a bit.

The problem was no longer the pandemic by itself that was keeping my husband awake at night and returning to his addictive nature, but it was the concerns of the next election that made things seem very bleak for him. He now felt as if the world might possibly be crumbling from underneath him all over again. I was doing everything I could to keep him upbeat and feeling positive. I was, once again, reminding him of everything we had together and how great our lives had become now that we were working together and keeping the devil at bay.

We never had another battle with each other, but we both continued to battle his need to rely on his addictive behaviors to see him through his frustrations and worries. We spoke of his health and how important it was for both of us to start focusing on our health and rebuilding ourselves physically into better shape.

Our love was strong, but I felt as if I was losing him; and somewhere inside of me, I started to feel as if I needed to absorb every bit of him all the time. I found myself consistently giving him affection and needing to take in everything about him, his scent, his laughter, his smile, and his touch; and it never seemed like I was absorbing enough. I did not take this as a sign of anything, not yet.

We continued to work and carry on, and the election was around the corner. The night of the election, I was sitting at my desk and suddenly noticed the sky outside. You really could not help but notice; the sky was emblazoned in the darkest blood-red sky I had ever seen. I was mesmerized by it. I took a picture and sent it to my husband, and he acknowledge his awareness of it.

As I drove home from work, I was in complete awe as to the blatant brightness of the red sky and how it seemed to cover every inch of the sky. It was like nothing I had ever seen. Still, I did not take this as a sign. I was missing the signs, or perhaps I was too scared to acknowledge what they might mean.

The election ended just the way my husband believed it would, and he began to spiral in anguish over the results.

Almost as quickly as he was angered and feeling down, he was deciding that he was not going to let this get to him, and he was going to be positive no matter what. He was going to remember our conversation and everything we had that mattered more than anything the world could throw at us. It was on one particular evening that he would look at me with such love in his eyes and tell me how beautiful I was and then look at our oldest boy and remind him to take good care of me if anything ever happened to him. I would find myself becoming concerned and remembering the previous occurrences that had taken place and thinking to myself that something did not seem right.

That evening, my husband did not seem at all like himself, and I could not place what was causing this change in him. I was not sure he understood it either. Early the next morning, he would leave to go and visit a friend after. I had stated that this did not seem necessary, and he should stay home. It was meant to be a short visit before his friend left for a trip out of town. After a length of time, I became nervous that he had not returned and attempted to call his phone; after the first few rings, a police officer answered his phone and informed me that my husband was found behind the wheel of his truck in a ditch on the side of the road, and he was nonresponsive.

The officer stated that he had performed CPR with no positive response and had sent him by EMS to the local hospital. My heart stood still, and the tears began to run down my face. I believed then that I had lost him forever.

I screamed for my third oldest who was staying with us that we needed to get to the hospital. I had to get there. I needed to try to be his saving grace once again. Upon arriving at the hospital, I was escorted to a small conference room by a young nurse, and I knew then, being a nurse myself and knowing the protocol, that my husband was never coming home to me again.

The doctor informed me that they were unable to save my husband as he confirmed my husband's death as a heart attack, and at that moment, I knew my life would never be the same again. A small part of me needed to confirm that they had the right person and that this was, in fact, my husband they had found and were unable to save. I was immediately taken to the ER where my husband lay, still warm to the touch but lifeless just the same.

I walked to his side, leaned over, and whispered in his ear, "I'm here, honey." I was hopeful that if he heard my voice, he might try to live. Of course, that hope quickly dissipated, and I knew it was time to say goodbye.

After kissing his cheek and telling him how much I loved him, I prayed over him with two of my sons by my side, all of us with tear-soaked faces and aching hearts. I prayed that the Lord would take his soul home, and he would find the peace he so very much deserved.

I was a complete mess and had no idea how I would ever go on without him.

Chapter 7

As I walked out of the hospital that night, I felt as if nothing seemed real anymore. I felt completely lost, almost like I was in a trance like the world was completely still; and I was walking through it all alone. I felt empty inside, like half of my soul was just ripped out. There was complete silence around me, or so it seemed. I could hear nothing, not one sound of the world moving around me. I must have called thirty people to tell them of my husband's death.

I had my second oldest flying home and my in-laws driving in that morning to endure this loss together, and the next step was telling my youngest. He was staying at a friend's house that night, and I needed to get him home and give him the heart-wrenching news that his dad had passed on.

My life was suddenly hell, and I could not lift a finger to fight my way out of it; and truthfully, I had no willpower to try. I could not feel a single part of my body. I could not sleep or eat, and there were times when I could not find my ability to breathe among the streaming tears. There were moments when I was screaming, "No! No! No!" while standing in the cold brisk air in the middle of my driveway, believing that if I continued to deny he was gone, it just might not be real! Of course, I was wrong.

My husband and I spent so much of our lives learning to manage his addictions and working to keep our marriage strong and our family whole. We neglected the most important need in all of this— our health. I have to believe that my husband's addictions as well as his diet, lack of exercise, and inability to deal with stress played a great part in his heart failure. He always seemed so full of life, like nothing could knock him down. He was physically strong and always bragged that he was healthier than most, and yet his body knew otherwise. The problem was, his body never told him; and if it did, he never told me.

It seemed unacceptable that at forty-nine years old, his life was over, and I was now a widow at forty-seven. The whole world was spinning around me while I remained lifeless and an emotional wreck.

I was angry at God. How could He choose this after we fought so hard all of our lives to beat all the bad, and finally, we had found each other again. We were happy. We were best friends. Our friendship and our love were stronger than ever. How could He just take him away? Why didn't I see the signs? The blood-red sky, the need to soak up every bit of my husband incessantly, the odd behavior he was displaying the night before. How did I miss it? Was God or my grandmother or both trying to distract me from the reality that was coming? Was there no chance I could have prevented this?

Every day, I find myself saying that I wish I would have realized the signs that were right in front of me. I wish there would have been physical warnings for him, and if there were, he would have told me. My husband had even shared with me a dream he had a couple of weeks prior to his death where he had lost control of his truck and went off the road. It freaked him out so much he refused to take a trip to the UP we had planned. Why did I not see into this? I did not even give it a second thought; I was just angry that we canceled the trip. I missed all the signs and heeded not one warning, and now he was gone—forever.

I have never been more scared and felt more lost and alone in all of my life. My boys stayed by my side every single day, making sure that I ate and that someone was there to catch me each time that I fell into uncontrollable sobbing and loss of breath and to coach me back into a calm, comforted state of being. I spent the next three months off work and trying to figure out what I needed to do next in my life. How was I going to get through all of this, and when was the pain going to go away? That is when I decided to write my husband a letter. I needed him to know I would be strong.

My dearest love,

A home once filled by you with music, laughter, and love is now empty, lost, and filled with anguish and heartbreak. You were far from perfect, and we were angered at you plenty, but you were the glue and the continued influence that kept our family whole. The passion that you held for keeping the family in touch and always sending love and making sure everyone was taken care of goes unmeasured, my love.

I look around our home, and I see an empty chair, an empty bed, and silence where you once beamed with constant random outbursts of words or songs or even sometimes orders barked with love. I see an empty desk where you sat to keep our lives in order financially and progressively to further our success in life.

I feel the emptiness not only in these four walls but also in my heart and within my soul.

I miss the warm smiles that greeted me home and the gentle hugs and kisses shared between us every day and throughout the day. I miss the desire to do something as a family and the question of, "What's the plans for the day? What's for din?"

I miss waking up to your beckons of, "Honey, time to get up." Your, "Good morning, sweetheart," with a smile that always melted my heart and a hug and kiss that always melted me completely. I miss the account of where we are and where we are headed. I miss tucking you in at night and you beckoning me to do so. I MISS YOU!

I miss the music playing throughout our home and your voice singing to every song, the beer brewing, and the way you lit up while you achieved a successful batch of the best beer ever made, at least we thought so.

I miss your arms around me, your confidence within me, and the way you always had the answers to everything. Even if I thought you were wrong, you believed eventually I would see you were right, and I hated admitting that you were right when I came to the realization that you were.

I miss your humor and your lightheartedness to every situation. I miss comforting you when you were frustrated or feeling letdown by life. I miss us as a team working together to achieve everything we worked for even if it was just cleaning the house and making a meal.

I miss your excitement when the boys would come home and when it was time to give you attention (foot rubs, back rubs, and me). I MISS YOU!

Our home is filled with silence now, and our hearts are filled with pain. Our lives will never be the same without you, and every moment that you filled with light and joy will be empty and void.

I know I cannot get you back, and I am sorry I did not make you stay. I am not sure why you were chosen to leave our world that day. I am still seeking those answers, and I am angry that you left me so soon and that our final moments were left undone. I miss you so much.

You were a beaming bright light in this world, and you filled so many lives with your glow. You have left a great impression on so many and now a hole in so many hearts with your absence. I pray you are at rest and at peace and that the Lord carried you home in comfort in His glorious arms.

> *I want you to know I will be strong, and I will never let you down. I will always love you; my heart will always belong to you, and I will always be proud of the lives we built together, the boys we raised, and the home we shared.*
>
> *You are forever my favorite boy in the whole world, and I cannot wait for the day I see you again at the heavenly gates of eternity. I am eternally yours, my love; and, babe, you are always in my heart.*
>
> *Rest well, my love, until we meet again in paradise.*

It was after this letter I started talking to my husband and God out loud. Every morning, I would sit on the porch with my coffee and share my thoughts with both of them. This was when I started to feel a sense of comfort and not so alone after all.

I am still doing this every morning, and I will probably never stop. I know that they are listening, and I too am listening with my heart for their guidance through the rest of my life.

It is now clear that I have to figure out what is next for me. All of my life I have been so busy fighting for everyone else that I have forgotten how to fight for myself. I have never taken the time to see who I was or what I wanted in life, and now I have no choice. I not only have to take over control of everything we once managed together, but I now also have to start over. I have to rebuild my life and learn who I am and what I want out of this next chapter in my life.

Have you ever found yourself in the midst of living your life just as you believed you were meant to, and then there's a sudden flash, and everything that once was just suddenly comes to a halt? Your world shifts on its axis, like you're part of some video game scenario or movie scene? You are now standing in the center of your life, feeling like everything is moving in slow motion and realizing, you are no longer on the same path that you once were. And you can't go back. The only option for you now is to start over.

So how do you start over from the middle of life you were already creating? You have already fallen in love with the boy of your dreams, and were high school sweethearts. You had the whole fairy tale wedding, have beautiful babies, and had begun your career in life; and now the next step was planning a life with the one you love after all of your kids have grown up and moved out to create their own path in life. Suddenly, the good Lord says, "Your story is going to change. I am taking the love of your life home with me." He then takes his golden pencil, erases the whole next chapter of your life, and says, "Start over, young lady. Find who you are and change your destiny."

Well, Lord, you are the author and the architect here. I am looking for your guidance now. I do not believe you have destined me to live the rest of my life alone, so I am counting on you to lead my heart in the right direction just as you did when I was fifteen. I am certain that there is some purpose for me in this world that leaves you changing my path in life because I feel that deep within my soul. So I will be here waiting for you to bring that to light for me. I can answer all the reasons for all the moves I made in the first chess game that led me to where I am today, but I am coming up quite empty with what my next move is on this suddenly-empty gameboard and what direction I am headed from here.

Falling in love is the easy part. You usually feel that deep in your heart the minute you see that perfect smile that makes the entirety of your internal self immediately become filled with warmth, and it lights you up from within. It's a conversation that is so easy it almost seems like they have always known you and an unstoppable force that will not allow you to stop thinking about them; and every time you do, it brings a smile to your face and happiness to your soul. You just somehow know they are the one.

The challenge is not in finding that person; the challenge is in finding you. The story does not start over until you figure out your next move where you are headed and what your ultimate destination in life really is.

Continuing your day-to-day life and working to pay the bills is just what's necessary, but it is not the answer. When God chooses to make changes in your life and turns the dial, forcing you to take another path, you are charged with the responsibility of choosing wisely and making every choice count.

You have to know within your heart and deep in your soul that he is expecting something special from you.

He chose for you to keep living for a reason, so open your mind, listen to your heart, and feel within your soul. Know that He will lead you toward your purpose on this earth, and He will fill you with all His blessings if you only choose to believe in Him.

I am not sure what my purpose is, and why He is choosing me to go on, and I have no clue where I am headed from here. But I am certain that wherever and whatever it is, the next move is mine to make. So I am clearing my mind so it is open for His direction, but I continue to remember what I once had; and I am opening my heart so I can feel new love while holding onto the greatest love. I am strengthening my soul so when the knock comes to my door, I can feel that what is meant for me is right while placing what once was tightly nestled in my memory. I will know that the Lord has chosen this new chapter for me because He still believes in me, and He sees a greater path for me than I am able to see for myself just yet!

Nobody ever says, "Prepare yourself for the possibility that one day your life will suddenly come to a halt, and everything you once knew will no longer be the same, and you will need to start a new journey on your own—all alone."

Everyone, when you experience this halt in life, says, "You are not alone. We are all here for you." But the simple fact is, they are not going to be in your every minute of everyday moments where you will be walking and falling until you find your strength and can confidently stand on your own alone.

It is a kind gesture to offer to be there for someone, but you must know that as comforting as those words seem, they fall short for the person you are offering them to because you quite simply cannot fill the gigantic void that is now present for them. You have your own lives to live. No, we, the people who are burdened with this new journey, must find our own path; and we must be responsible for filling the gaps now present in our lives.

After working a few more months at my current job, I realized this was no longer where I was meant to be. I needed to move on. I needed time to heal and to find my purpose in life. I reached out to God and asked Him to lead me there. It was then that I found the need to write this book and share with all of you the story of our lives and the hurdles we climbed in hopes to provide a different perspective on how you, too, can fight through the storm, beat the odds, and find your positive outcome through it all.

It has been almost a year since I lost the love of my life, and my entire lifetime suddenly came to an end. It amazes me how easily the days go by, and we continue to move further and further away from that fateful day—the day when my heart broke into two, and my sanctity of comfort and forever love was gone in the blink of an eye. A relationship written in the stars found a meteor that blasted out its soul but will never burn out its light.

I spend most of my days wearing a smile that hides the pain in my heart and serves as a cover for the tears that I shed privately on my own. Throughout every day, there arise moments where I am reminded that my sweet love is gone; and of the many reasons that I miss him, I have found that I am no longer the same person. I have lost a great deal of who I used to be, someone in love, someone filled with confidence and reassurance that I would always be okay, a woman who had everything she needed and was beyond happy with everything in her life. A woman who knew that there was no one in the world that she wanted more than the man she was so lucky to have.

I am now walking blindly through each day, swinging at the obstacles flying in my path and taking on responsibilities that were never before left for me to worry about because my husband took care of these things without even a second's thought every day.

I feel a certain burning in my soul that yearns for everything to return to normal and all of this to be a horrible nightmare that I suddenly wake up from and hope never to return to again.

I lay in bed staring at his picture, sharing my day with him and asking him why he was chosen to leave so soon. I sometimes find myself screaming at him and angrily telling him about the mess he left me in. I tell him how his boys and I miss him dearly and of all the things he is missing that are occurring each and every day. I spitefully tell him how I bought a new car because they took his away, and how I am doing things to please me because I deserve something better than the pain he left me to feel; and yet, secretly I am hoping that the things I am doing are making him proud.

It is funny how all of sudden in the middle of a day while at work or driving home and most times at the end of a night when I am climbing into my empty bed I have a brief epiphany that he is really gone and not coming home. It seems crazy that I seem to keep forgetting this or perhaps keep telling myself internally that none of this is real.

It is said in the bible that God allows suffering to bring us closer to Him. As much as I love the idea of being closer to God, I pray He reaches out to comfort me and ease my pain very soon.

I pray that He guides my boys through their lives and keeps them safe and sound, strong and smart, healthy, and happy. I do this every night in hopes that He continues to watch over our family and to be the security we lost when we lost our dad and husband so recently, so unexpectedly, and so young.

I am not sure this pain will ever go away, and somedays, I hope it does not for fear of it becoming a past. I do not ever want my husband to be someone in my past but, instead, to be forever in my heart and a feeling that remains in my soul and my mind always. I know I will always see him in the faces and personalities of my children. I will never forget how happy he made me the day he chose me to be his one and only, and I can see him still the night before he died, staring at me and telling our boys, "Look at her. Look how beautiful she is. Make sure you always take care of her." For a split second, I wondered why he said such a thing but then quickly dismissed it as something he always said to our boys, "When I am gone, you boys make sure you take care of your mom."

I miss him, I miss his smile, I miss his voice and his laughter, I miss his hugs, and I miss his passion for music, for brewing beer, for hot summer days, for early mornings, and for loving his family and friends.

I miss my husband every single minute of every day. It has been almost a year, and it feels like an eternity; and with that, a whole life still to go on without him.

I am filled with a new and different strength I have never endured before. It's one that enables me to be mom and dad, to be the sole provider and the widowed wife, a term I despise, and a single woman in print but never in my heart.

I am burdened with never forgetting and never wanting to but crying out in frustration that I cannot fix this; I cannot correct it or take it back or prevent it from ever happening.

I am chosen to suffer and challenged to survive once again, and I am reminded that I can do all things through Christ who strengthens me.

Strengthen me, Lord, and help me find serenity within my pain. I hope one day I will find it all well within my soul.

Chapter 8

Yes, I know my story's outcome does not seem all that positive at the moment. I lost the love of my life, my reason for being so willing to fight through the trenches, my teammate through it all. It would seem our fighting was futile and a waste of time. It would seem we lost after all, but that is simply not true. We won!

My husband left this world knowing how loved he was and leaving me more in love with him than ever. He knew the mountains we had climbed and the victories we had achieved. He knew the risk he had taken with the choices he made and the impurities he had put into his body all his life, and he was proud of the strength he had found to resist the worst of it. Yes, sir, we were the greatest team ever, and we were champions to each other and to our children; and nothing matters more than that. My husband has quite simply completed his journey here on earth, and I am left to continue mine.

What I can tell you is that all of those years of battling each other and my husband's addictions were all worth it. They were not easy years, and there is still hurt that has not gone away. But now having lost him, those hurtful moments do not seem to register with me, and I can only remember the best moments with him. I can only see him as a beautiful soul that I was madly in love with. I truly learned a great deal from our battles throughout our lives together. The greatest of those things I learned was that we came through it all because we let God and our love lead us.

If I take from what the Lord is sharing with me and the feeling I am getting from His guidance, everyone has a journey to fulfill. We all have a purpose through God on this earth, and only He truly knows what the purpose is and how our journey is supposed to carry out before He offers us a place in His kingdom and allows us an opportunity to ask for His forgiveness for the mistakes we made along the way, providing us a pathway to walk with Him in paradise.

Having had my heart filled with this belief, I am aware that my journey must continue, and I must carry on. I must fulfill what God has chosen for me to do on this earth, and if I open my heart and my mind and allow Him to lead me, I will never be misdirected. My life will be filled with the glory of His love, patience, and understanding. I, too, will find my place in paradise where I will once again meet up with my sweet husband in all of his heavenly beauty.

If there is one thing I am learning from all of the recent occurrences in my life, it is that I have never taken the time to stop and really see the world around me and all of the glory my Lord has provided for me. What I have seen is that our world and the leaders in it have enveloped themselves in a cesspool of greed, manipulation, and an overwhelming desire for control. In the midst of becoming aware of all of these things as well as the loss of my husband, it has become apparent that all of us need to stop, completely shut out all of our needs, our desires, and our day-to-day routines and just sit down on our lawn, our porch, the beach, wherever we are and just take in all of God's beauty around us.

We simply need to smell the sweet air, see the beauty in the trees, the flowers, the birds, the grass, and the water. We need to look up at the sky and smile at the shades of blue and the soft white clouds, feel the sunshine on our face, and remember that this is what life is, not the money we are making, not the job we are doing, not the house or the car or even the clothes on our back. It is not just another day; it is every day that this exists, and all of us are missing it and all of its glory because we are too busy trying to do what society has programmed us to do.

We are missing life, folks, because we are choosing greed, power, and luxury. I stopped what I was doing one day, and I said, "Life is too short to be locked up in a building, staring at a screen, and being beat up by someone else's frustrations." It was then I stepped away from my position and said, "I am going to go and find peace within myself and with my life through the Lord. I am going to watch my son grow, and I am going to sit back and watch the world bustle around me and remember the real beauty in this world and the reason it exists, the real meaning of life." I am beyond blessed because I found that today.

As I sat among the beauty of the Lord and became totally enveloped within it. I was captured by the true serene of the trees and the green grass. I smelled the sweetness of the air and felt the breeze caressing my hair. I looked up and smiled at the deep blue sky, and I saw the stairway to heaven within the glorious white, fluffy clouds and the golden rays of the sun. And it was then I felt an amazing sense of peace and was truly blessed. I am happy for my husband and the glory he has found, and I am elated to be alive and blessed to feel love deep within my soul and to know that I am loved. I feel hope again. I feel happiness again, and I know that this is the real life, the life God wants us to live. This is the only life for me.

Don't let the beauty of life pass you by. Let go of the worries. Let go of the day-to-day and just sit back and find your fullness in life before it is too late, and you have missed the real purpose of life.

God does not want you to struggle. He does not want you to be burdened and angry and exhausted. He wants you to remember Him and have faith in Him and live for Him and through Him. He wants you to know that through Him, life is glorious and easy. It's full of sweet air and sunshine and soft breezes every day. Do not live for what society programs you to believe you need. Live for what God believes you need, and He will fill your life and soul with everything you need to live a glorious life.

I know I told you early on that I was not here to preach to you or place my faith in you, and I am not. I am here to share with you how wonderful it feels to feel fullness in your life and to take in all of the wondrous beauty of God's creation around you and really see it every day. I want you all to feel that way too. I want our world to stop feeling like desperate hope and treacherous letdowns and to start remembering. We do not need any of these earthly goods to make life beautiful. We already have all the treasures in the world surrounding us each day. We just need to stop and take it all in and let the rest fall behind us and away from us. That's how we change the world, that's how we take back our lives, and that's how we find peace in our souls and happiness in our hearts.

Life will never be easy until you allow it to be easy. You will always have hurdles to climb, rivers to cross, and demons to fight, but if you let go of the willingness to let it get to you and let God take it all over, you will see that it cannot affect you anymore because nothing in this earthly world is stronger than the will of God. If you love someone, show them you love them, be there for them, stand beside them, and trudge the rough waters with them for as long as you can. If they stop trudging and lose the fight, know that you gave it all you had and that you loved them all the while. It is not always your fight to fight, but it is your heart that you must answer to and your mind that will seek peace when all is said and done.

Someone very special to me reminded me that "peace is only from within yourself. You always have it in you. If the outside world is lacking the peace you seek, just go inside yourself to bring it out. It is a choice to let others drag you down. Do not let them." If you know that you did everything you could, and you never gave up, then you did good. Remember, God has a reason and a purpose for all of us, and only He knows when your time has come to bear no more, and only He chooses when it is time to come home.

I know I never gave up fighting for our marriage, our family, and our lives; and I know I loved my husband until the absolute end and still do and always will. I know I will see him again one day, and when I do, I will never let go. I won't have to.

It took me thirty-three years to come to the realization that I was not to blame for my husband's pain or his reason for his reliance on his addictions. I sometimes still find myself feeling as if I let him down somehow as if I am letting my children and myself down with my decisions today and every day. Have you ever suddenly felt like you have let everyone down in your life? Like the world is just too hard? Have you ever found yourself holding everyone to high expectations in life and then turned around, looked in the mirror, and realized you are no longer meeting your own set level of expectations?

Have you ever sat alone in a room and realized that just when you thought you were strong and had the world by the tail, you do not?

Every day is that day for me. I sent my youngest son off to his first day of junior high, and for the first time in my life, I did not have a job to go to. On my return home, I felt a bit strange, but it was after arriving home that I felt completely and utterly lost and letdown by myself. I realized I have no purpose. I am placing all of these expectations on my children and someone I care a great deal about, and who am I? I am asking someone to stop and change their whole life for me and for who?

For someone who has no idea what her next step is, for someone who just wants to run away from the whole world and sit by a body of water and cry to God that she is a failure, for someone who gave up when life got too hard, I honestly have no drive to go back to work as a nurse, at least not in the same way; and I have absolutely no idea where I am headed or what life has in store for me.

I loved having a partner, someone I could pull strength from, someone I could share frustrations with, someone who could hold me when I was hurting. I know I am a strong woman, and I am capable of anything I set my mind to, but I am strong to a fault. I hold strength in being a mom because I genuinely love being a mom, and I love my boys with all of my heart.

I hold strength in being a wife and a partner because I love caring for someone and loving someone, and I cherish affection and intimacy. I am a strong daughter because I love my mom and want to do everything I can to care for her, but my strength in myself is only based on how well all of those titles are performed by me.

I honestly do not know how to be strong for me. I have never been given the moment to care for myself and decide what I want or what makes me happy. I do not know how to manage life all on my own, and I am not sure I want to. So I concluded today that I have reached failure.

I have failed to ever live my life for me. I have failed at reaching true independence, and I have failed to hold strong for myself. I possess the greatest strength in loving others, building others up, and caring for others, especially my children. I live my life through my love of others. When I give you my love, my love is true, loyal, and unconditional. I have failed to love me. I have failed to truly see who I am and what I mean to myself. Today, I am choosing to love myself; and if someone loves me again, they must understand that I am worth loving, and I am worth the choices they may have to choose in order to be with me. They may not have seen this coming, but they better be ready to take a leap for me because I am no longer willing to be the only one leaping unless it's for me!

I have reached failure, failure in seeing my own worth and in living my life for me; but I am not a failure, and I am not weak. I am strong, I am smart, and I am worth the challenge. I am worth someone climbing mountains to be with me and to care for me. It is my turn to live my life for me! This is what I have learned today after so many challenging days in the past.

For those of you who share in some of the same struggles I have, you must remember to live for yourself. Find who you are and what you want out of your life and this world and reach to the good Lord. Let Him know you are ready to listen and to be heard. Stand strong and say, "World, you have not met me yet, but you are going to love me when you do!" Do not find yourself failing. Find yourself reaching for all of your desires, but reach for them through the Lord's vision for you, and you will see them all fall into place as they should.

Chapter 9

Now I must start my journey over. I must find myself in this world and who I want to be on this second start I have been given. I could never have imagined how much I would be responsible for if placed in a position of living on my own. I now have a home full of thirty-two years of memories and mementos, collections, and treasures. I am lost in a swarm of what do I do with this? How can I make new moves with all of this baggage behind me? So I am downsizing, and I am weeding out what is valuable and what was simply pieces that seemed important at that time but suddenly now have little value in my life.

I have determined that the most valuable treasures in my life are my children, my family, and the people I hold dear in my life. I am discovering that I no longer want to be the person I once was, but I want to be better. I want to live my life full of purpose and excitement and for me! I am challenging myself to want more. I want passion. I want happiness. I want freedom, and I still want love. Yes, believe it or not, it is still hard for me to believe, but I want to love again. I do not choose to continue on in this world alone.

I deserve to love and be loved, and I know my husband would want that for me too. I know I would have wanted it for him should the roles have been reversed.

What I am aiming for now is a change. I do not want to be the same nurse I once was, working for an organization and following their every command. I am not sure I want to be a nurse at all. What I am sure of is that I want to help others. I want to be a source of inspiration, encouragement, and compassion for others. I once lived my life to care for others and respond to all of their needs, but now I want to care for others by helping them see their worth and their strength in themselves and in the Lord.

I know this will not come easy and that I will endure many challenges and battles before all is said and done. I do not have much money, and I am currently without health insurance. But I cannot back down, and I cannot give in to this materialistic world and watch my desires go unmet once again. My children are less than thrilled over my life choices these days, but I have spent my whole life making the best choices for them and others, and now they must learn to understand and appreciate my choices for me because I will not give in to what others believe is best for me anymore. What is best for me will be decided by me and only me.

I have spent the last ten months saying goodbye to my previous life, kissing the soft cheek of my dear husband, holding his hand, and saying goodbye to our life together on this earth and through all the pain and anguish, learning that life is short, and you must live and live now, enjoy every moment, and be happy. And the only one who truly makes that happen is you.

I truly believed after my husband died that there would be no one else for me and that I only had love for one man, and he was gone.

Now I am learning that quite possibly that is just simply not true. I am learning that the good Lord gives you a heart that allows many forms of love and to always be able to love again. I know that my love for my husband will never go away, and he will always be my forever love and my favorite boy in all the world, and loving again will never diminish or relinquish that.

My life and my decisions are now what is on the table and the matter at hand. I have battled marriage woes, spousal addictions, and the trials of my dear mother and raised children; but now it is my turn, and I am ready to live for me and set my sights on the life ahead of me. I have never been in this situation before, and I am scared but excited to see how happy I can make myself, and how much I can make my desires a reality. I want to walk in faith and follow God's lead. I want to help others to find that inner peace they have been searching for, and I want to tell God's story and share mine in hopes that I can turn one frown into a smile, light up one set of eyes, melt one heart, and carry one soul home to paradise.

I am not looking to create miracles or part the Red Sea. I am merely looking to show compassion, provide encouragement, and spread love and hope. I want to see a better world transpire, one where we do not feel treacherous remorse and spiteful letdowns that send us spiraling out of control.

I want to see a world that does not find us searching for answers in a bottle or a pill or a powder but allows us to find the answers within ourselves and through our Lord, not our government.

My husband did not get that opportunity. He lost his hope for a better world, and he left our world knowing we had not found peace yet, and I am grateful that he has now found his peace. He is living in paradise surrounded by hope and love and walking in the glory of the Lord. If there is one thing my husband taught us all, it was when given the reigns, take control. These weren't his exact words, but at the risk of sharing someone else's sentiment, you get the picture. My children have done just that, and now it is my turn.

I am not sure where my path takes me from here, or where I will end up in the working end of things; but what I can take with me for certain is that I have loved, I have battled, I have struggled, I have climbed, and I have fallen and found myself standing again and standing stronger than ever before. I know what it feels like to hurt, to feel pain and anguish, and to feel loss and suffering; and more than anything, I know how it feels to find faith, peace, happiness, and love.

I can feel pride in the life my husband and I shared and the family we raised, and I know without any uncertainty that he is watching over us, and he is proud of how we are carrying on in light of his passing. I am elated to start my next chapter in life, and I cannot wait to share it with all of you.

If there is one thing that I can give to all of you who are going through a loss of a loved one, whether it is a spouse, a child, a family member, or even a dear friend or if you are just enduring a difficult time in your life, there is only one way I have managed to get through this last year and see myself past the hurt, the anguish, the pain, the anger, the frustrations, and the want to just give up with the belief that I could not live in this world without my husband, that was through my faith in the Lord.

I know without a doubt that the Lord is by my side, that He has walked me through so many trials and tribulations in my lifetime, and that He never gives up on me; and I refused to give up on Him. Therefore, I will never give up on myself. I will always do as my beautiful grandmothers taught me, and I will put all of my faith, my troubles, and my love in God's hands; and I know he will see me through. I know he has a plan for me, and I cannot wait to see what that plan holds.

I hope with all my heart that it holds everything I am dreaming of, and while He works, I will talk with Him every day. I will reassure Him that I am not giving up on this life, and I am not giving up on myself. I am not giving up on my dreams. I am not giving up on my family. I am not giving up on this world, and I will not give up on finding love.

I will keep fighting for myself, for my children, for my family, and for God. I want to share with all of you how wonderful our Lord is, how He will never let you down, and how He will walk you through every storm if you just believe. I promise you He has walked me through so many storms, and the answers are not always what I want to hear, but He is always right in the end.

I want all of you to feel that feeling of peace and solitude in your lives. I want you to know that you are never alone. He is always with you if you allow Him to be.

Don't give up, don't lose hope, and never lose faith. You will get through the storm, and life will go on. So do yourself a favor and know that you never have to move on, but you must keep on. The challenges in life are never easy, and the losses hurt like hell; but if we place our faith in the Lord and find within us the resilience to get back up and keep on, we can make our journey truly worthwhile.

About the Author

K. L. Nelson is a Christian woman who has found herself touched by the spiritual world and is passionate about her faith and her love of writing. She started writing publicly last year in a personal opinion blog entitled *KristaBell's Ponders and Possibilities* after a college professor admired her work and encouraged her to share it with others. You can find these additional writings at kristabells-ponders.com. She is a licensed registered nurse and a very blessed mother of four incredible children. Her hope is to inspire in faith and to motivate others to be warriors and see that through great will and determination, we can think outside of the boxes that we have created for ourselves and be greater than we ever imagined. She believes if we learn to live our lives through God and His guidance, we will find our journey in life to be a rewarding and peaceful one.

9 798888 540220